C000162153

ISBN 978-0-260-05529-3
PIBN 11023134

1 MONTH OF
FREE
READING

at
www.ForgottenBooks.com

By purchasing this book you are eligible for one month membership to ForgottenBooks.com, giving you unlimited access to our entire collection of over 1,000,000 titles via our web site and mobile apps.

To claim your free month visit:
www.forgottenbooks.com/free1023134

ENGLISH Housewifery.

EXEMPLIFIED
In above FOUR HUNDRED AND FIFTY

RECEIPTS,

Giving DIRECTIONS in most Parts of

COOKERY;

And how to prepare various SORTS of

SOOPS,	CAKES,
MADE-DISHES,	CREAMS,
PASTES,	JELLIES,
PICKLES,	MADE-WINES, &c.

With CUTS for the orderly placing the DISHES and COURSES; also BILLS OF FARE for every Month in the Year; and an alphabetical INDEX to the Whole.

A Book necessary for Mistresses of Families, higher and lower Women Servants, and confined to Things USEFUL, SUBSTANTIAL and SPLENDID, and calculated for the Preservation of HEALTH, and upon the Measures of FRUGALITY, being the Result of thirty Years PRACTICE and EXPERIENCE.

By ELIZABETH MOXON.

WITH AN

APPENDIX,

Containing upwards of Seventy RECEIPTS, of the most valuable Kind, (many never before printed) communicated to the Publisher by several Gentlewomen in the Neighbourhood, distinguished by their extraordinary Skill in HOUSEWIFERY.

The TENTH EDITION, CORRECTED.

LEEDS: Printed by GRIFFITH WRIGHT:

THE
PREFACE.

*I*T is not doubted, but the candid Reader will find the following *BOOK* in correspondence with the title, which will supersede the necessity of any other recommendation that might be given it.

As the compiler of it engaged in the undertaking at the instance and importunity of many persons of eminent account and distinction, so she can truly assure them, and the world, that she has acquitted herself with the utmost care and fidelity.

And she entertains the greater hopes that her performance will meet with the kinder acceptance, because of the good opinion she has been held in by those, her ever honour'd friends, who first excited her to the publication of her *BOOK*, and who have been long eye-witnesses of her skill and behaviour in the business of her calling.

She has nothing to add, but her humblest thanks to them, and to all others from whom she has received favour and encouragement.

THE
PREFACE.

English HOUSEWIFERY.

1. *To make* VERMICELLY SOOP.

TAKE a neck of beef, or any other piece; cut off some slices, and fry them with butter 'till they are very brown; wash your pan out every time with a little of the gravy; you may broil a few slices of the beef upon a gridiron: put all together into a pot, with a large onion, a little salt, and a little whole pepper; let it stew 'till the meat is tender, and skim off the fat in the boiling; then strain it into your dish, and boil four ounces of vermicelly in a little of the gravy 'till it is soft: Add a little stew'd spinage; then put all together into a dish, with toasts of bread; laying a little vermicelly upon every toast. Garnish your

A   dish

diſh with creed rice and boil'd ſpinage, or carrots flic'd thin.

2. Cucumber Soop.

Take a houghill of beef, break it ſmall, and put it into a ſtew-pan, with part of a neck of mutton, a little whole pepper, an onion, and a little ſalt ; cover it with water, and let it ſtand in the oven all night, then ſtrain it and take off the fat ; pare ſix or eight middle-ſiz'd cucumbers, and ſlice them not very thin, ſtew them in a little butter and a little whole pepper; take them out of the butter and put 'em into the gravy. Garniſh your diſh with raſpings of bread, and ſerve it up with toaſts of bread or *French* roll.

3. *To make* Hare Soop.

Cut the hare into ſmall pieces, waſh it and put it into a ſtew-pan, with a knuckle of veal ; put in it a gallon of water, a little ſalt, and a handful of ſweet herbs ; let it ſtew 'till the gravy be good ; fry a little of the hare to brown the ſoop ; you may put in it ſome cruſts of white bread among the meat to thicken the ſoop ; put it into a diſh, with a little ſtew'd ſpinage, criſp'd bread, and a few forc'd-meat balls. Garniſh your diſh with boil'd ſpinage and turnips, cut it in thin ſquare ſlices.

4. *To make Green* Pease Soop.

Take a neck of mutton, and a knuckle of veal, make of them a little good gravy ; then take half a peck of the greeneſt young

peaſe,

peafe, boil and beat them to a pulp in a marble mortar; then put to them a little of the gravy; ftrain them through a hair fieve to take out all the pulp; put all together, with a little falt and whole pepper; then boil it a little, and if you think the foop not green enough, boil a handful of fpinage very tender, rub it through a hair-fieve, and put into the foop, with one handful of wheat flour, to keep it from running: You muft not let it boil after the fpinage is put in, it will difcolour it; then cut white bread in little diamonds, fry them in butter while crifp, and put it into a difh, with a few whole peafe. Garnifh your difh with creed rice, and red beet-root.

You may make afparagus-foop the fame way, only add tops of afparagus, inftead of whole peafe.

5. To make ONION SOOP.

Take four or five large onions, peel and boil them in milk and water whilft tender, (fhifting them two or three times in the boiling) beat 'em in a marble mortar to a pulp, and rub them thro' a hair-fieve, and put them into a little fweet gravy; then fry a few flices of veal, and two or three flices of lean bacon; beat them in a marble mortar as fmall as forc'd-meat; put it into your ftew-pan with the gravy and onions, and boil them; mix a fpoonful of wheat-flour with a little water, and put it into the foop to keep it

from

from running; ſtrain all through a cullender, ſeaſon it to your taſte; then put into the diſh a little ſpinage ſtew'd in butter, and a little criſp bread; ſo ſerve it up.

6. *Common* Pease Soop *in Winter.*

Take a quart of good boiling peaſe which put into a pot with a gallon of ſoft water whilſt cold; add thereto a little beef or mutton, a little hung beef or bacon, and two or three large onions; boil altogether while your ſoop is thick; ſalt it to your taſte, and thicken it with a little wheat-flour; ſtrain it thro' a cullender, boil a little ſellery, cut it in ſmall pieces, with a little criſp bread, and criſp a little ſpinage as you would do parſley, then put it in a diſb, and ſerve it up. Garniſh your diſh with raſpings of bread.

7. *To make* Pease Soop *in Lent.*

Take a quart of peaſe, put them into a pot with a gallon of water, two or three large onions, half a dozen anchovies, a little whole pepper and ſalt; boil all together whilſt your ſoop is thick; ſtrain it into a ſtew-pan through a cullender, and put fix ounces of butter (work'd in flour) into the ſoop to thicken it; alſo put in a little boil'd ſellery, ſtew'd ſpinage, criſp bread, and a little dry'd mint powdered; ſo ſerve it up.

8. Craw-Fish Soop.

Take a knuckle of veal, and part of a neck of mutton to make white gravy, putting in an onion, a little whole pepper and

ſalt

falt to your tafte ; then take twenty craw-
fifh, boil and beat them in a marble mortar,
adding thereto a little of the gravy ; ftrain
them and put them into the gravy ; alfo
two or three pieces of white bread to thicken
the foop ; boil twelve or fourteen of the
fmalleft craw-fifh, and put them whole into
the difh, with a few toafts, or *French* roll,
which you pleafe ; fo ferve it up.

You may make lobfter foop the fame way,
only add into the foop the feeds of the lobfter.

9. *To make* SCOTCH SOOP.

Take an houghill of beef, cut it in pieces,
with part of a neck of mutton, and a pound
of *French* barley ; put them all into your pot,
with fix quarts of water ; let it boil 'till the
barley be foft, then put in a fowl ; as foon
as 'tis enough put in a handful of red beet
leaves or broccoli, a handful of the blades
of onions, a handful of fpinage, wafhed and
fhred very fmall ; only let them have a little
boil, elfe it will fpoil the greennefs. Serve
it up with the fowl in a difh, garnifh'd with
rafpings of bread.

10. *To make* SOOP *without Water.*

Take a fmall leg of mutton, cut it in
flices, feafon it with a little pepper and falt ;
cut three middling turnips in round pieces,
and three fmall carrots fcrap'd and cut in pieces, a handful of fpinage, a little parfley, a
bunch of fweet herbs, and two or three cabbage lettice ; cut the herbs fmall, lay
a row of meat and a row of herbs ; put the

tur-

turnips and carrots at the bottom of the pot
with an onion, lay at the top half a pound
of fweet butter, and clofe up the pot with
coarfe pafte; then put the pot into boiling
water, and let it boil for four hours; or in
a flow oven, and let it ftand all night; when
it is enough drain the gravy from the meat,
fkim off the fat, then put it into your difh
with fome toafts of bread, and a little ftew'd
fpinage; fo ferve it up.

11. *To ftew a* BRISKET *of* BEEF.

Take the thin part of a brifket of beef,
fcore the fkin at the top; crofs and take off
the under fkin, then take out the bones, feafon it highly with mace, a little falt, and a
little whole pepper, rub it on both fides, let
it lay all night, make broth of the bones, fkim
the fat clean off, put in as much water as will
cover it well, let it ftew over a flow fire four
or five hours, with a bunch of fweet herbs
and an onion cut in quarters; turn the beef
over every hour, and when you find it tender take it out of the broth and drain it very
well, having made a little good ftrong gravy.

A ragout with fweet-breads cut in pieces,
pallets tenderly boil'd and cut in long pieces;
take truffles, morels and mufhrooms, if you
have any, with a little claret, and throw in
your beef, let it ftew a quarter of an hour in
the ragout, turning it over fometimes, then
take out your beef, and thicken your ragout
with a lump of butter and a little flour.
Garnifh your difh with horfe-radifh and
pickles,

pickles, lay the ragout round your beef, and
a little upon the top ; fo ferve it up.

12. To ftew a RUMP of BEEF.

Take a fat rump of young beef and cut off
the fag end, lard the low part with fat bacon,
and ftuff the other part with fhred parfley ;
put it into your pan with two or three quarts
of water, a quart of claret, two or three
anchovies, an onion, two or three blades of
mace, a little whole pepper, and a bunch of
fweet herbs ; ftew it over a flow fire five or
fix hours, turning it feveral times in the
ftewing, and keep it clofe cover'd ; when
your beef is enough take from it the gravy,
thicken part of it with a lump of butter and
flour, and put it upon the difh with the
beef. Garnifh the difh with horfe-radifh
and red-beet root. There muft be no falt
upon the beef, only falt the gravy to your
tafte.

You may ftew part of a brifket, or an ox
cheek the fame way.

13. To make OLIVES of BEEF.

Take fome flices of a rump (or any other
tender piece) of beef, and beat them with a
pafte pin, feafon them with nutmeg, pepper
and falt, and rub them over with the yolk
of an egg ; make a little forc'd meat of veal,
beef-fuet, a few bread crumbs, fweet-herbs,
a little fbred mace, pepper, falt, and two
eggs, mixed all together ; take two or three
flices of the beef, according as they are in

A 4 bignefs,

bignefs, and a lump of forc'd-meat the fize
of an egg; lay your beef round it, and roll it
in part of a kell of veal, put it into an earth-
en difh, with a little water, a glafs of claret,
and a little onion fhred fmall; lay upon them
a little butter, and bake them in an oven a-
bout an hour; when they come out take off
the fat, and thicken the gravy with a little
butter and flour; fix of them is enough for
a fide difh. Garnifh the difb with horfe-
radifh and pickles.

You may make olives of veal the fame
way.

14. *To fry* BEEF - STEAKS.

Take your beef fteaks and beat them with
the back of a knife, fry them in butter over
a quick fire, that they may be brown before
they be too much done; when they are enough
put them into an earthen pot whilft you have
fry'd them all; pour out the fat, and put
them into your pan with a little gravy, an
onion fhred very fmall, a fpoonful of catchup and a little falt; thicken it with a little
butter and flour, the thicknefs of cream.
Garnifh your difh with pickles.

Beef-fteaks are proper for a fide-difh.

15. BEEF - STEAKS *another Way.*

Take your beef-fteaks and beat them with
the back of a knife, ftrow them over with a
little pepper and falt, lay them on a gridiron
over a clear fire, turning 'em whilft enough;
fet your difh over a chafing-difb of coals,

with

with a little brown gravy ; chop an onion
or fhalot as fmall as pulp, and put it a-
mongft the gravy ; (if your fteaks be not over
much done, gravy will come therefrom;) put
it on a difh and fhake it all together. Garnifh your difb with fhalots and pickles.

16. *A* Shoulder *of* Mutton *forc'd.*

Take a pint of oyfters and chop them, put
in a few bread-crumbs, a little pepper, fhred
mace, and an onion, mix them all together,
and ftuff your mutton on both fides, then
roaft it at a flow fire, and bafte it with nothing but butter; put into the dripping-pan
a little water, two or three fpoonfuls of the
pickle of oyfters, a glafs of claret, an onion
fhred fmall, and an anchovy ; if your liquor
wafte before your mutton is enough, put
in a little more water ; when the meat is
enough, take up the gravy, fkim off the fat,
and thicken it with flour and butter ; then
ferve it up. Garnifh your dilh with horfe-
radifh and pickles.

17. *To ftew a* Fillet *of* Mutton.

Take a fillet of mutton, ftuff it the fame
as for a fhoulder, half roaft it, and put it into a ftew pan with a little gravy, a jill of
claret, an anchovy, and a fhred onion ; you
may put in a little horfe-radifh. and fome
mufhrooms ; ftew it over a flow fire while
the mutton is enough ; take the gravy, fkim
off the fat, and thicken it with flour and
butter ; lay forc'd-meat balls round the mut-

A 5

ton.

ton. Garniſh your diſh with horſe-radiſh
and muſhrooms.

It is proper either for a ſide-diſh or bottom
diſb ; if you have it for a bottom-diſh, cut
your mutton into two fillets.

18. *To Collar a* BREAST *of* MUTTON.

Take a breaſt of mutton, bone it, and ſeaſon it with nutmeg, pepper and ſalt, rub it
over with the yolk of an egg ; make a little
forc'd-meat of veal or mutton, chop it with
a little beef-ſuet, a few bread-crumbs, ſweet
herbs, an onion, pepper and ſalt, a little
nutmeg, two eggs, and a ſpoonful or two
of cream ; mix all together and lay it over
the mutton, roll it up and bind it about with
coarſe incle ; put it into an earthen diſh
with a little water, dridge it over with flour,
and lay upon it a little butter ; it will require
two hours to bake it. When it is enough,
take up the gravy, ſkim off the fat, put in
an anchovy and a ſpoonful of catchup, thick-
en it with flour and butter ; take the incle
from the mutton and cut it into three or four
rolls ; pour the ſauce upon the diſh, and
lay about it forc'd-meat balls. Garniſh your
diſh with pickles.

It is either proper for a ſide or bottom-
diſh.

19. *To Collar a* BREAST *of* MUTTON, *ano-*
ther Way.

Take a breaſt of mutton, bone it, and ſeaſon it with nutmeg, pepper and ſalt ; roll

it

it up tight with coarfe incle and toaft it upon
a fpit ; when it is enough lay it whole upon
the difh. Then take four or fix cucumbers,
pare them and cut them in flices, not very
thin ; likewife cut three or four in quarters
length way, ftew them in a little brown
gravy and a little whole pepper; when they
are enough, thicken them with flour and butter the thicknefs of cream ; fo ferve it up.
Garnifh your difh with horfe-radifh.

20. *To Carbonade a* BREAST *of* MUTTON.

Take a breaft of mutton, half bone it, nick
it crofs, feafon it with pepper and falt ; then
broil it before the fire whilft it be enough,
ftrinkling it over with bread-crumbs ; let the
fauce be a little gravy and butter, and a
few fhred capers ; put it upon the difh with
the mutton. Garnifh it with horfe-radifh
and pickles.

This is proper for a fide-difh at noon, or
a bottom-difb at night.

21. *A Chine of* MUTTON *roafted, with ftew'd* SELLERY.

Take a loyn of mutton, cut off the thin
part and both ends, take off the fkin, and
feore it in the roafting as you would do pork;
then take a little fellery, boil it, and cut it
in pieces about an inch long, put to it a little good gravy, whole pepper and falt, two
or three fpoonfuls of cream and a lump of
butter, fo thicken it up, and pour it upon

A 6. your

'your dish with your mutton.————This is proper for a side-dish.

22. Mutton-Chops.

Take a leg of mutton half-roasted, when it is cold cut it in thin pieces as you would do any other meat for hashing, put it into a stew-pan with a little water or small gravy, two or three spoonfuls of claret, two or three shalots shred, or onions, and two or three spoonfuls of oyster pickle ; thicken it up with a little flour, and so serve it up. Garnish your dish with horse-radish and pickles.

You may do a shoulder of mutton the same way, only boil the blade-bone, and lic in the middle.

23. *A forc'd* Leg *of* Mutton.

Take a leg of mutton, loose the skin from the meat, be careful you do not cut the skin as you loosen it ; then cut the meat from the bone, and let the bone and skin hang together, chop the meat small, with a little beef suet, as you would do sausages ; season it with nutmeg, pepper and salt, a few bread-crumbs, two or three eggs, a little dry'd sage, shred parsley and lemon-peel ; then fill up the skin with forc'd meat, and lay it upon an earthen dish ; lay upon the meat a little flour and butter, and a little water in the dish ; it will take an hour and a half baking ; when you dish it up lay about it either mutton or veal collops, with brown gravy sauce. Garnish your dish with horse-radish

radiſh and lemon. You may make a forc'd leg of lamb the ſame way.

24. *To make* FRENCH CUTLETS *of* MUTTON.

Take a neck of mutton, cut it in joints, cut off the ends of the long bones, then ſcrape the meat clean off the bones about an inch, take a little of the inpart of the meat of the cutlets, and make it into forc'd meat; ſeaſon it with nutmeg, pepper and ſalt; then lay it upon your cutlets, rub over them the yolk of an egg to make it ſtick; chop a few ſweet herbs, and put to them a few bread-crumbs, a little pepper and ſalt, and ſtrew it over the cutlets, and wrap them in double writing-paper; either broil them before the fire or in an oven, half an hour will do them; when you diſh them up, take off the out-paper, and ſet in the midſt of the diſb a little brown gravy in a china baſon; you may broil them without paper, if you pleaſe.

25. *To fry* MUTTON STEAKS.

Take a loyn of mutton, cut off the thin part, then cut the reſt into ſteaks, and flat them with a bill, ſeaſon them with a little pepper and ſalt, fry them in butter over a quick fire; as you fry them put them into a ſtew-pan or earthern pot, whilſt you have fried them all; then pour the fat out of the pan, put in a little gravy, and the gravy that comes from the ſteaks, with a ſpoonful of claret, an anchovy, and an onion or a ſhalot

lot fhred; fhake up the fteaks in the gravy, and thicken it with a little flour; fo ferve them up. Garnifh your difh with horfe radifh and fhalots.

26. To make artificial VENISON of MUTTON.

Take a large fboulder of mutton, or a middling fore quarter, bone it, lay it in an earthen difh, put upon it a pint of claret, and let it lie all night; when you put it into your pafty-pan or difh, pour on the claret that it lay in, with a little water and butter; before you put it into your pafty-pan, feafon it with pepper and falt; when you make the pafty lie no pafte in the bottom of the difh.

27. How to brown Ragout a BREAST of VEAL.

Take a breaft of veal, cut off both the ends, and hàlf roaft it; then put it into a ftew-pan, with a quart of brown gravy, a fpoonful of mufhroom-powder, a blade or two of mace and lemon-peel; fo let it ftew over a flow fire while your veal is enough; then put in two or three fhred mufhrooms or oyfters, two or three fpoonfuls of white wine; thicken up your fauce with flour and butter; you may lay round your veal fome ftew'd morels and truffles; if you have none, fome pallets ftew'd in gravy, with artichoke-bottoms cut in quarters, dipt in eggs and fry'd, and fome forc'd-meat balls; you may fry the fweet-bread cut in pieces, and lay over the veal, or fry'd oyfters; when you fry

your.

your oyfters you muft dip them in egg and flour mixed. Garnifh your difh with lemon and pickles.

28. *A Herico of a* BREAST *of* VEAL, French *Way.*

Take a breaft of veal, half roaft it, then put it into a ftew - pan, with three pints of brown-gravy; feafon your veal with nutmeg, pepper and falt; when your veal is ftew'd enough, you may put in a pint of green peafe boil'd. Take fix middling cucumbers, pare and cut them in quarters long way, alfo two cabbage-lettices, and ftew them in brown gravy; fo lay them round your veal when you difh it up, with a few forc'd-meat-balls and fome flices of bacon. Garnifh your difh with pickles, mufhrooms, oyfters and lemons.

29. *To roll a* BREAST *of* VEAL.

Take a breaft of veal, and bone it, feafon it with nutmeg, pepper and falt, rub it over with the yolk of an egg, then ftrew it over with fweet herbs fhred fmall, and fome flices of bacon, cut thin to lie upon it, roll it up very tight, bind it with coarfe incle, put it into an earthen difh with a little water, and lay upon it fome lumps of butter; ftrew a little feafoning on the outfide of your veal, it will take two hours baking; when it is baked take off the incle and cut it in four rolls, lay it upon the difh with a good brown gravy-fauce: lay about your veal the fweat-bread

fry'd

fry'd, some forc'd-meat-balls, a little crisp
bacon, and a few fry'd oysters if you have
any ; so serve it up. Garnish your dish with
pickles and lemon.

30. *A stew'd* BREAST *of* VEAL.

Take the fattest and whitest breast of veal
you can get, cut off both ends and boil them
for a little gravy ; take the veal and raise up
the thin part, make a forc'd-meat of the
sweet-bread boil'd, a few bread crumbs, a
little beef suet, two eggs, pepper and salt,
a spoonful or two of cream, and a little nutmeg, mix'd all together ; so stuff the veal,
skewer the skin close down, dridge it over
with flour, tie it up in a cloth, and boil
it in milk and water about an hour. For
the sauce take a little gravy, about a jill of
oysters, a few mushrooms shred, a little lemon shred fine, and a little juice of lemon ;
so thicken it up with flour and butter ; when
you dish it up pour the same over it ; lay over
it a sweet-bread or two cut in slices and fry'd,
and fry'd oysters. Garnish your dish with
lemon, pickles and mushrooms.

This is proper for a top dish either at noon
or night.

31. *To stew a* FILLET *of* VEAL.

Take the leg of the best whye veal, cut
off the dug and the knuckle, cut the rest into two fillets, and take the fat part and cut
it in pieces the thickness of your finger ; you
must stuff the veal with the fat ; make the

hole

hole with a penknife, draw it thro' and fkewer it round, feafon it with pepper, falt, nutmeg, and fbred parfley; then put it into your ftew-pan, with half a pound of butter, (without water) and fet it on your ftove; let it boil very flow and cover it clofe up, turning it very often; it will take about two hours in ftewing; when it is enough pour the gravy from it, take off the fat, put into the gravy a pint of oyfters and a few capers, a little lemon peel, a fpoonful or two of white wine, and a little juice of lemon; thicken it with butter and flour the thicknefs of cream; lay round it forc'd-meat-balls and oyfters fry'd, and fo ferve it up. Garnifh your difh with a few capers and flic'd lemon.

32. *To make* SCOTCH COLLOPS.

Take a leg of veal, take off the thick part, cut it in thin flices for collops, beat them with a pafte-pin 'till they be very thin; feafon them with mace, pepper and falt; fry them over a quick fire, not over brown; when they are fried put them into a ftew-pan with a little gravy, two or three fpoonfuls of white wine, two fpoonfuls of oyfter-pickle if you have it, and a little lemon-peel; then fhake them over a ftove in a ftew-pan, but don't let them boil over much, it only hardens your collops; take the fat part of your veal, ftuff it with forc'd-meat, and boil it; when it is boiled lay it in the middle of your difh with the collops; lay about your col-

lops

lops flices of crifp bacon, and forc'd - meat
balls. Garnifh your difh with flices of lemon and oyfters, or mufhrooms.

33. *To make* VEAL CUTLETS.

Take a neck of veal, cut it in joints, and
flatten them with a bill; cut off the ends of
the bones, and lard the thick part of the cutlets with four or five bits of bacon; feafon it
with nutmeg, pepper and falt; ftrew over
them a few bread crumbs, and fweet herbs
fbred fine; firft dip the cutlets in egg to
make the crumbs ftick, then broil them before the fire, put to them a little brown gravy
fauce, fo ferve it up. Garnifh your difh
with lemon.

34. VEAL CUTLETS *another Way.*

Take a neck of veal, cut it in joints, and
flat them as before, and cut off the ends of
the long bones; feafon them with a little
pepper, falt and nutmeg, broil them on a
gridiron, over a flow fire; when they are
enough, ferve them up with brown gravy
fauce and forc'd-meat balls.
Garnifh your difh with lemon.

35. VEAL CUTLETS *another Way.*

Take a neck of veal and cut it in flices,
flatten them as before, and cut off the ends
of the long bones; feafon the cutlets with
pepper and falt, and dridge over them fome
flour; fry them in butter over a quick fire;
when they are enough put from them the fat
they were fried in, and put to them a little

fmall

small gravy, a spoonful of catchup, a spoonful of white wine or juice of lemon, and
grate in some nutmeg; thicken them with
flour and butter, so serve them up.

Garnish your dish as before.

36. *To Collar a* CALF's HEAD *to eat hot.*

Take a large fat head, and lay it in water
to take out the blood; boil it whilst the bones
will come out; season it with nutmeg, pepper and salt; then wrap it up round with a
large lump of forc'd meat made of veal;
after which wrap it up tight in a veal kell before it is cold, and take great care that you
don't let the head break in two pieces; then
bind it up with a coarse incle, lay it upon an
earthen dish, dridge it over with flour,
and lay over it a little butter, with a little
water in the dish; an hour and a half will
bake it; when it is enough take off the incle,
cut it in two length ways, laying the skin-
side uppermost; when you lay it upon your
dish you must lay round it stew'd pallets
and artichoke-bottoms fry'd with forc'd-meat
balls; put to it brown gravy-sauce; you
may brown your sauce with a few truffles or
morels, and lay them about your veal.

Garnish your dish with lemon and pickle.

37. *To Collar a* CALF's HEAD *to eat cold.*

You must get a calf's head with the skin
on, split it and lay it in water, take out the
tongue and eyes, cut off the groin ends,
then tie it up in a cloth and boil it whilst the

bones

bones come out; when it is enough lay it on
a table with the fkin-fide uppermoft, and
pour upon it a little cold water; then take
off the hair and cut off the ears; mind you
do not break the head in two, turn it over
and take out the bones; falt it very well and
wrap it round in a cloth very tight, pin it with
pins, and tie it at both ends, fo bind it up
with broad incle, then hang it up by one end,
and when it is cold take it out; you muft
make for it brown pickle, and it will keep
half a year; when you cut it, cut it at the neck.

It is proper for a fide or middle difh, either for noon or night.

38. *To make a* CALF's HEAD *Hafh.*

Take a calf's head and boil it, when it
is cold take one half of the head and cut off
the meat in thin flices, put it into a ftew-pan
with a little brown gravy, put to it a fpoonful or two of walnut pickle, a fpoonful of
catchup, a little claret, a little fhred mace,
a few capers fhred, or a little mango; boil it
over a ftove, and thicken it with butter and
flour; take the other part of the head,
cut of the bone ends and fcore it with a knife,
feafon it with a little pepper and falt, rub it
over with the yolk of an egg, and ftrew over
a few bread crumbs, and a little parfley; then
fet it before the fire to broil whilft it is brown;
and when you difh up the other part lay this
in the midft; lay about your hafh brain-
cakes, forc'd-meat balls and crifp bacon.

To make Brain-cakes ; take a handful of bread - crumbs, a little fhred lemon - peel, pepper, falt, nutmeg, fweet-marjorum, parfley fhred fine, and the yolks of three eggs ; take the brains and fkin them, boil and chop them fmall, fo mix them all together; take a little butter in your pan when you fry them, and drop them in as you do fritters, and if they run in your pan put in a handful more of bread-crumbs.

39. *To hafh a* CALF's HEAD *white.*

Take a calf's head and boil it as much as you would do for eating, when it is cold cut it in thin flices, and put it into a ftew-pan with a white gravy ; then put to it a little fhred mace, falt, a pint of oyfters, a few fhred mufhrooms, lemon-peel, three fpoonfuls of white wine, and fome juice of lemon, fhake all together, and boil it over the ftove, thicken it up with a little flour and butter ; when you put it on your difh, you muft put a boil'd fowl in the midft, and a few flices of crifp bacon.

Garnifh your difh with pickles and lemon.

40. *A Ragout of a* CALF's HEAD.

Take two calves' heads and boil them as you do for eating, when they are cold cut off all the lantern part from the fiefh in pieces above an inch long, and about the breadth of your little finger; put it into your ftew-pan with a little white gravy ; twenty oyfters cut in two or three pieces, a few fhred mufh-

rooms,

rooms, and a little juice of lemon; feafon it
with fhred mace and falt, let them all boil
together over a ftove; take two or three
fpoonfuls of cream, the yolks of two or three
eggs, and a little fhred parfley, then put it
into a ftew-pan; after you have put the cream
in you may fhake it all the while; if you let
it boil it will curdle, fo ferve it up.

Garnifh your difh with fippets, lemon,
and a few pickled mufhrooms.

41. *To roaft a* CALF's HEAD *to eat like Pig.*

Take a calf's head, wafh it well, lay it
in an earthen difh, and cut out the tongue,
lay it loofe under the head in the difb with
the brains, and a little fage and parfley; rub
the head over with the yolk of an egg,
then ftrew over them a few bread-crumbs
and fhred parfley, lay all over it lumps of
butter and a little falt, then fet in the oven;
it will take about an hour and a half baking;
when it is enough take the brains, fage and
parfley, and chop them together, put to them
the gravy that is in the difh, a little butter
and a fpoonful of vinegar, fo boil it up and
put it in cups, and fet them round the head
upon the difh, take the tongue and blanch
it, cut it in two, and lay it on each fide the
head, and fome flices of crifp bacon over
the head, fo ferve it up.

42. SAUCE *for a* NECK *of* VEAL.

Fry your veal, and when fried put in a
little water, an anchovy, a few fweet herbs,
a little

a little onion, nutmeg, a little lemon-peel fhred fmall, and a little white wine or ale, then fhake it up with a little butter and flour, and fome cockles and capers.

43. To boil a Leg of Lamb, with the Loyn fry'd about it.

When your lamb is boil'd lay it in the difb, and pour upon it a little parfley, butter and green goofeberries coddled, then lay your fried lamb round it; take fome fmall afparagus and cut it fmall-like peafe, and boil it green; when it is boil'd drain it in a cullender, and lay it round your lamb in fpoonfuls.

Garnifh your difh with goofeberries, and heads of afparagus in lumps.

This is proper for a bottom difb.

44. A Leg of Lamb boil'd with Chickens round it.

When your lamb is boil'd pour over it parfley and butter, with coddled goofeberries, fo lay the chickens round your lamb, and pour over the chickens a little white fricafſy fauce. Garnifh your difh with fippets and lemon.

This is proper for a top difh.

45. A Fricaſſee of Lamb white.

Take a leg of lamb, half roaft it, when it is cold cut it in flices, put it into a ftew-pan with a little white gravy, a fhalot fhred fine, a little nutmeg, falt, and a few fhted capers; let it boil over the ftove whilft the lamb is enough; to thicken your fauce, take three

fpoonfuls

spoonfuls of cream, the yolks of two eggs, a little shred parsley, and beat them well together, then put it into your stew-pan and shake it whilst it is thick, but don't let it boil; if this do not make it thick, put in a little flour and butter, so serve it up. Garnish your dish with mushrooms, oysters and lemon.

46. *A brown Fricassee of* LAMB.

Take a leg of lamb, cut it in thin slices and season it with pepper and salt, then fry it brown with butter, when it is fried put it into your stew-pan, with a little brown gravy, an anchovy, a spoonful or two of white wine or claret, grate in a little nutmeg, and set it over the stove; thicken your sauce with flour and butter. Garnish your dish with mushrooms, oysters and lemon.

47. *To make* PIG *eat like* LAMB *in Winter.*

Take a pig about a month old and dress it, lay it down to the fire, when the skin begins to harden you must take it off by pieces, and when you have taken all the skin off, draw it, and when it is cold cut it in quarters and lard it with parsley; then roast it for use.

48. *How to stew a* HARE.

Take a young hare, wash and wipe it well, cut the legs into two or three pieces, and all the other parts the same bigness, beat them all flat with a paste-pin, season it with nutmeg and salt, then flour it over, and fry it in butter over a quick fire; when you have fried

it

it put it into a ſtew-pan, with about a pint of
gravy, two or three ſpoonfuls of claret and
a ſmall anchovy, ſo ſhake it up with butter
and flour, (you muſt not let it boil in the
ſtew-pan, for it will make it cut hard) then
ſerve it up. Garniſh your diſb with criſp
parſley.

49. *How to Jug a* Hare.

Take a young hare, cut her in pieces as
you did for ſtewing, and beat it well, ſeaſon
it with the ſame ſeaſoning you did before, put
it into a pitcher or any other cloſe pot, with
half a pound of butter, ſet it in a pot of boiling water, ſtop up the pitcher cloſe with a
cloth, and lay upon it ſome weight for fear
it ſhould fall on one ſide ; it will take about
two hours in ſtewing ; mind your pot be
full of water, and keep it boiling all the
time ; when it is enough take the gravy from
it, clear off the fat, and put her into your
gravy in a ſtew-pan, with a ſpoonful or two
of white wine, a little juice of lemon, ſhred
lemon-peel and mace ; you muſt thicken it
up as you would a white fricaſſee.

Garniſh your diſh with ſippets and lemon.

50. *To roaſt a* Hare *with a pudding in the belly.*

When you have waſh'd the hare, nick the
legs in the joints, and ſkewer them on
both ſides, which will keep her from drying
in the roaſting ; when you have ſkewer'd her,
put the pudding into her belly, baſte her
with nothing but butter : put a little water
in the dripping pan ; you muſt not baſte it

B   with

with the water at all : when your hare is enough, take the gravy out of the dripping pan, and thicken it up with a little flour and butter for the fauce.

How to make a Pudding for the Hare.

Take the liver, a little beef-fuet, fweet-marjoram and parfley fhred fmall, with bread-crumbs and two eggs; feafon it with nutmeg, pepper and falt to your tafte, mix all together and if it be too ftiff put in a fpoonful or two of cream : You muft not boil the liver,

51. To make a brown fricaffee of RABBETS.

Take a rabbet, cut the legs in three pieces each, and the remainder of the rabbet the fame bignefs, beat them thin and fry them in butter over a quick fire; when they are fried put them into a ftew-pan with a little gravy, a fpoonful of catchup, and a little nutmeg; then fhake it up with a little flour and butter.

Garnifh your difh with crifp parfley.

52. A white fricaffee of RABBETS.

Take a couple of young rabbets and half roaft them ; when they are cold take off the fkin, and cut the rabbets in fmall pieces, (only take the white part) when you have cut it in pieces, put it into a ftew-pan with white gravy, a fmall anchovy, a little onion, fhred mace and lemon-peel, fet it over a ftove, and let it have one boil, then take a little cream, the yolks of two eggs, a lump of butter, a little juice of lemon and fhred

parfley;

parfley; put them all together into a ftew-
pan, and fhake them over the fire whilft
they be as white as cream; you muft not let
it boil, if you do it will curdle. Garnifh your
difb with fbred lemon and pickles.

53. *How to make pulled* RABBETS.

Take two young rabbets, boil them very
tender, and take off all the white meat, and
pull off the fkin, then pull it all in fhives,
and put it into your ftew-pan with a little
white gravy, a fpoonful of white wine, a
little nutmeg and falt to your tafte; thicken
it up as you would a white fricaffee, but put
in no parfley; when you ferve it up lay the
heads in the middle. Garnifh your difh
with fhred lemon and pickles.

54. *To drefs Rabbets to look like* MOOR-GAME.

Take a young rabbet, when it is cafed cut
off the wings and the head; leave the neck
of your rabbet as long as you can; when you
cafe it you muft leave on the feet, pull off
the fkin, leave on the claws, fo double your
rabbet and fkewer it like a fowl; put a
fkewer at the bottom through the legs and
neck, and tie it with a ftring, it will prevent
its flying open; when you difh it up make
the fame fauce as you would do for partridges.
Three are enough for one difh.

55. *To make white* SCOTCH COLLOPS.

Take about four pounds of a fillet of veal,
cut it in fmall pieces as thin as you can, then
take a ftew-pan, butter it well over, and

fhake

fhake a little flour over it, then lay your
meat in piece by piece, whilft all your pan be
covered ; take two or three blades of mace,
and a little nutmeg, fet your ftew-pan over
the fire, tofs it up together 'till all your meat
be white, then take half a pint of ftrong veal
broth, which muft be ready made, a quarter
of a pint of cream, and the yolks of two
eggs, mix all thefe together, put it to your
meat, keeping it toffing all the time 'till
they juft boil up, then they are enough ; the
laft thing you do fqueeze in a little lemon :
You may put in oyfters, mufhrooms, or
what you will to make it rich.

56. *To boil* Ducks *with* Onion Sauce.

Take two fat ducks, feafon them with
a little pepper and falt, and fkewer them up
at both ends, and boil them whilft they are
tender ; take four or five large onions and
boil them in milk and water, change the
water two or three times in the boiling,
when they are enough chop them very fmall,
and rub them through a hair-fieve with the
back of a fpoon, 'till you have rubb'd them
quite through, then melt a little butter,
put in your onions and a little falt, and pour
it upon your ducks. Garnifh your difh
with onions and fippets.

57. *To ftew* Ducks *either wild or tame.*

Take two ducks and half roaft them, cut
them up as you would do for eating, then
put them into a ftew-pan with a little brown
gravy,

gravy, a glaſs of claret, two anchovies, a ſmall onion ſhred very fine, and a little ſalt ; thicken it up with flour and butter, ſo ſerve it up. Garniſh your diſh with a little raw onion and ſippets.

58. To make a white fricaſſee of CHICKENS.

Take two or more chickens, half-roaſt them, cut them up as you would do for eating, and ſkin them ; put them into a ſtew-pan with a little white gravy, juice of lemon, two anchovies, ſhred mace and nutmeg, then boil it ; take the yolks of three eggs, a little ſweet cream and ſhred parſley, put them into your ſtew-pan with a lump of butter and a little ſalt ; ſhake them all the while they are over the ſtove, and be ſure you do not let them boil leſt they ſhould curdle. Garniſh your diſh with ſippets and lemon.

59. How to make a brown fricaſſee of CHICKENS.

Take two or more chickens, as you would have your diſh in bigneſs, cut them up as you do for eating, and flat them a little with a paſte-pin ; fry them a light brown, and put them into your ſtew-pan with a little gravy, a ſpoonful or two of white wine, a little nutmeg and ſalt ; thicken it up with flour and butter. Garniſh your diſh with ſippets and criſp parſley.

60. CHICKENS SURPRISE.

Take half a pound of rice, ſet it over a fire in ſoft water, when it is half boiled put in two or three ſmall chickens truſs'd, with

two

two or three blades of mace, and a little
falt ; take a piece of bacon about three inches
fquare, ánd boil it in water whilft almoft
enough, then take it out, pare off the out
fides, and put it into the chickens and rice
to boil a little together ; (you muft not let
the broth be over thick with rice) then
take up your chickens, lay them on a difh,
pour over them the rice, cut your bacon in
thin flices to lay round your chickens, and
upon the breaft of each a flice.

This is proper for a fide-difh.

61. *To boil* CHICKENS.

Take four or five fmall chickens, as you
would have your difh in bignefs ; if they be
fmall ones you may fcald them, it will make
them whiter ; draw them, and take out the
breaft bone before you fcald them ; when you
have drefs'd them, put them into milk and
water, and wafh them, trufs them, and cut
off the heads and necks ; if you drefs them
the night before you ufe them, dip a cloth
in milk and wrap them in it, which will
make them white ; you muft boil them in
milk and water, with a little falt ; half an
hour or lefs will boil them.

To make Sauce for the CHICKENS.

Take the necks, gizzards and livers, boil
them in water, when they are enough ftrain
off the gravy, and put to it a fpoonful of
oyfter-pickle ; take the livers, break them
fmall, mix a little gravy, and rub them
through

through a hair-fieve with the back of a fpoon, then put to it a fpoonful of cream, a little lemon and lemon-peel grated; thicken it up with butter and flour. Let your fauce be no thicker than cream, which pour upon your chickens. Garnifh your difh with fip-pets, mufhrooms, and flices of lemon.

They are proper for a fide-difh or a top-difh either at noon or night.

62. *How to boil a* Turkey.

When your turkey is drefs'd and drawn, trufs her, cut off her feet, take down the breaft-bone with a knife, and few up the fkin again; ftuff the breaft with a white ftuffing.

How to make the Stuffing. Take the fweet-bread of veal, boil it, fhred it fine, with a little beef-fuet, a handful of bread-crumbs, a little lemon-peel, part of the liver, a fpoon-ful or two of cream, with nutmeg, pepper, falt, and two eggs; mix all together, and ftuff your turkey with part of the ftuffing, (the reft you may either boil or fry to lay round it) dredge it with a little flour, tie it up in a cloth, and boil it in milk and water : If it be a young turkey an hour will boil it.

How to make Sauce for the Turkey. Take a little fmall white gravy, a pint of oyfters, two or three fpoonfuls of cream, a little juice of lemon, and falt to your tafte, thicken it up with flour and butter, then pour it over your turkey, and ferve it up; lay round your turkey fry'd oyfters, and the forc'd-meat.

Garnifh

Garnifh your difh with oyfters, mufhrooms, and flices of lemon.

63. *How to make another Sauce for a* Turkey.

Take a little ftrong white gravy, with fome of the whiteft fellery you can get, cut it about an inch long, boil it whilft it be tender, and put it into the gravy, with two anchovies, a little lemon-peel fbred, two or three fpoonfuls of cream, a little fhred mace, and a fpoonful of white wine; thicken it up with flour and butter; if you diflike the fellery you may put in the liver as you did for chickens.

64. *How to roaft a* TURKEY.

Take a turkey, drefs and trufs it, then take down the breaft-bone. *To make Stuffing for the Breaft.* Take beef-fuer, the liver fhred fine and bread-crumbs, a little lemon-peel, nutmeg, pepper and falt to your tafte, a little fhred parfley, a fpoonful or two of cream, and two eggs. Put her on a fpit and roaft her before a flow fire; you may lard your turkey with fat bacon; if the turkey be young, an hour and a quarter will roaft it. For the fauce, take a little white gravy, an onion, a few bread-crumbs, and a little whole pepper, let them boil well together, put to them a little flour and a lump of butter, which pour upon the turkey; you may lay round your turkey forc'd-meat balls.

Garnifh your difb with flices of lemon.

65. *To make a rich* TURKEY PIE.

Take a young turkey and bone it, only
leave

leave in the thigh bones and ſhort pinions ; take a large fowl and bone-lt, a little ſhred mace, nutmeg, pepper and ſalt, and ſeaſon the turkey and fowl in the inſide ; lay the fowl in the inſide of the low part of the tur⸱key, and ſtuff the breaſt with a little white ſtuffing, (the ſame white ſtuffing as you made for the boiled turkey,) take a deep diſb, lay a paſte over it, and leave no paſte in the bottom ; lay in the turkey, and lay round it a few forc'd-meat balls, put in half a pound of butter, and a jill of water, then cloſe up the pie, an hour and a half⸱ will bake it ; when it comes from the oven take off the lid, put in a pint of ſtew'd oyſters, and the yolks of fix or eight eggs, lay them at equal diſtances round the turkey ; you muſt not ſtew your oyſters in gravy but in water, and pour them upon your turkey's breaſt ; lay round fix or eight artichoke-bottoms fry'd, ſo ſerve it up without the lid ; you muſt take the fat out of the pie before you put in the oyſters.

66. *To make a* TURKEY *A-la-Daube.*

Take a large turkey and trufs it ; take down the breaſt-bone, and ſtuff it in the breaſt with ſome ſtuffing, as you did the roaſt turkey, lard it with bacon, then rub the ſkin of the turkey with the yolk of an egg, and ſtrew over it a little nutmeg, pepper, ſalt, and a few bread-crumbs, then put it into a copper-diſb and ſend it to the oven ; when you diſb it up make for the turkey brown gravy-ſauce ;

ſhred

fhred into your fauce a few oyfters and
mufhrooms ; lay round artichoke-bottoms
fry'd, ftew'd pallets, forc'd-meat balls, and
a little crifp bacon. Garnifh your difh with
pickled mufhrooms, and flices of lemon.

This is a proper difh for a remove.

67. POTTED TURKEY.

Take a turkey, bone her as you did for
the pie, and feafon it very well in the infide
and outfide with mace, nutmeg, pepper and
falt, then put it into a pot that you defign
to keep it in, put over it a pound of butter,
when it is baked draw from it the gravy, and
take off the fat, then fqueeze it down very
tight in the pot ; and to keep it down lay upon it a weight ; when it's cold take part of
the butter that came from it, and clarify a little more with it to cover your turkey, and
keep it in a cool place for ufe ; you may
put a fowl in the belly if you pleafe.

Ducks or geefe are potted the fame way.

68. *How to jugg* PIGEONS.

Take fix or eight pigeons and trufs them,
feafon them with nutmeg, pepper and falt.
To make the Stuffing. Take the livers and
fhred them with beef-fuet, bread-crumbs, parfley, fweet-marjoram, and two eggs, mix all
together, then ftuff your pigeons fowing them
up at both ends, and put them into your jugg
with the breaft downwards, with half a pound
of butter ; ftop up the jugg clofe with a cloth
that no fteam can get out, then fet them in

a pot

a pot of water to boil ; they will take about two hours ftewing ; mind you keep your pot full of water, and boiling all the time ; when they are enough clear from them the gravy, and take the fat clean off ; put to your gravy a fpoonful of cream, a little lemon-peel, an anchovy fhred, a few mufhrooms, and a little white wine, thicken it with a little flour and butter, then difh up your pigeons, and pour over them the fauce. Garnifh the difh with mufhrooms and flices of lemon.

This is proper for a fide difb.

69. MIRRANADED PIGEONS.

Take fix pigeons, and trufs them as you would do for baking, break the breaft-bones, feafon and ftuff them as you did for jugging, put them into a little deep difh and lay over them half a pound of butter ; put into your difb a little water. Take half a pound of rice, cree it foft as you would do for eating, and pour it upon the back of a fieve, let it ftand while it is cold, then take a fpoon and flat it like pafte on your hand, and lay on the breaft of every pigeon a cake ; lay round your difh fome puff-pafte not over thin, and fend them to the oven ; about half an hour will bake them.

This is proper at noon for a fide difh.

70. To ftew PIGEONS.

Take your pigeons, feafon and ftuff them, flat the breaft-bones, and trufs them up as you

B 6 would

would do for baking, dredge them over with
a little flour, and fry them in butter, turning them round till all fides be brown, then
put them into a ftew-pan with as much brown
gravy as will cover them, and let them ftew
whilft your pigeons be enough ; then take
part of the gravy, an anchovy fhred, a little
catchup, a fmall onion, or a fhalot, and a
little juice of lemon for fauce, pour it over
your pigeons, and lay round them forc'd-
meat balls and crifp bacon. Garnifh your
difh with crifp parfley and lemon.

71. To broil PIGEONS whole.

Take your pigeons, feafon and ftuff them
with the fame ftuffing you did jugg'd pigeons,
broil them either before a fire or in an oven ;
when they are enough take the gravy from
them, and take off the fat, then put to the
gravy two or three fpoonfuls of water, a
little boil'd parfley fhred, and thicken your
fauce. Garnifh your difb with crifp parfley.

72. Boiled PIGEONS with fricaffee fauce.

Take your pigeons, and when you have
drawn and trufs'd them up, break the breaft-
bones, and lay them in milk and water to
make them white, tie them in a cloth and
boil them in milk and water ; when you difh
them up put to them white fricaffee fauce, only adding a few fhred mufhrooms. Garnifh
with crifp parfley and fippets.

73. To pot PIGEONS.

Take your pigeons and fkewer them with
their

their feet crofs over the breaft, to ftand up ;
feafon them with pepper and falt, and roaft
them ; fo put them into your pot, fetting the
feet up ; when they are cold cover them up
with clarified butter.

74. *To ftew* PALLETS.

Take three or four large beaft pallets and
boil them very tender, blanch and cut them
in long pieces the length of your finger, then
in fmall bits the crofs way ; fhake them up
with a little good gravy and a lump of butter ; feafon them with a little nutmeg and
falt, put in a fpoonful of white wine, and
thicken it with the yolks of eggs as you do
a white fricaffee.

75. *To make a fricaffee of* PIG's EARS.

Take three or four pig's ears, according as
you would have your difh in bignefs, clean
and boil them very tender; cut them in fmall
pieces the length of your finger, and fry
them with butter till they be brown ; fo put
them into a ftew-pan with a little brown
gravy, a lump of butter, a fpoonful of vinegar, and a little muftard and falt, thicken'd
with flour ; take two or three pig's feet and
boil them very tender, fit for eating, then
cut them in two and take out the large bones,
dip them in egg, and ftrew over them a few
bread-crumbs, feafon them with pepper and
falt ; you may either fry or broil them, and
lay them in the middle of your difh with
the pig's ears.

They

They are proper for a side-dish.

76. *To make a Fricassee of* TRIPES.

Take the whiteft feam tripes you can get, and cut them in long pieces, put them into a ftew-pan with a little good gravy, a few bread-crumbs, a lump of butter, a little vinegar to your tafte, and a little muftard if you like it; fhake it up altogether with a little fhred parfley. Garnifh your difh with fippets.

This is proper for a fide-difh.

77. *To make a Fricassee of* VEAL SWEET-BREADS.

Take five or fix veal fweet breads, according as you would have your difh in bignefs, and boil them in water, cut them in thin flices the length way, dip them in egg, feafon them with pepper and falt, fry them a light brown; then put them into a ftew-pan with a little brown gravy, a fpoonful of white wine or juice of lemon, whether you pleafe; thicken it up with flour and butter; and ferve it up. Garnifh your difh with crifp parfley.

78. *To make a white Fricassee of* TRIPES, *to eat like* CHICKENS.

Take the whiteft and the thickeft feam tripe you can get, cut the white part in thin flices, put it into a ftew-pan with a little white gravy, juice of lemon and lemon-peel fhred, alfo a fpoonful of white wine; take the yolks of two or three eggs and beat them very well, put to them a little thick cream, fhred parfley,

fley, and two or three chives if you have any ; fhake altogether over the ftove while it be as thick as cream, but don't let it boil for fear it curdle. Garnifh your difh with fip-pets, fliced lemon or mufhrooms, and ferve it up.

79. *To make a brown Fricaſſee of* Eggs.

Take eight or ten eggs, according to the bigneſs you defign your difh, boil them hard, put them in water, take off the fhell, fry them in butter whilft they be a deep brown, put them into a ftew-pan with a little brown gravy, and a lump of butter, fo thicken it up with flour ; take two or three eggs, lay them in the middle of the difh, then take the other, cut them in two, and fet them with the fmall ends upwards round the difb ; fry fome fippets and lay round them. Garnifh your difh with crifp parfley.

This is proper for a fide-difh in lent or any other time.

80. *To make a white Fricaſſee of* Eggs.

Take ten or twelve eggs, boil them hard and peel them, put them in a ftew-pan with a little white gravy ; take the yolks of two or three eggs, beat them very well, and put to them two or three fpoonfuls of cream, a fpoonful of white wine, a little juice of le-mon, fhred parfley, and falt to your tafte ; fhake all together over the ftove 'till it be as thick as cream, but don't let it boil ; take **your**

your eggs and lay one part whole on the difh, the reft cut in halves and quarters, and lay them round your difh ; you muft not cut them till you lay them on the difh. Garnifh your difb with fippets, and ferve it up.

81. *To ftew* EGGS *in* GRAVY.

Take a little gravy, pour it into a little pewter difh, and fet it over a ftove, when it is hot break in as many eggs as will cover the difh bottom, keep pouring the gravy over them with a fpoon 'till they are white at the top, when they are enough ftrew over them a little falt ; fry fome fquare fippets of bread in butter, prick them with the fmall ends upward, and ferve them up.

They are proper for a fide difb at fupper.

82. *How to Collar a Piece of* BEEF *to eat Cold.*

Take a flank of beef or pale-bone, which you can get, bone it and take off the inner fkin ; nick your beef about an inch diftance, but mind you don't cut thro' the fkin of the outfide ; then take two ounces of faltpetre, and beat it fmall, and take a large handful of common falt and mix them together, firft fprinkling your beef over with a little water, and lay it in an earthen difh, then ftrinkle over your falt, fo let it ftand, four or five days, then take a pretty large quantity of all forts of mild fweet herbs, pick and fhred them very fmall, take fome bacon and cut it in long pieces the thicknefs of your finger, then take your beef and lay one layer of

bacon

bacon in every nick ; and another of the
greens ; when you have done feafon your
beef with a little beat mace, pepper, falt and
nutmeg; you may add a little neat's tongue,
and an anchovy in fome of the nicks ; fo roll
it up tight, bind it in a cloth with coarfe incle
round it, put it into a large ftew-pot and cover it with water; let the beef lie with the
end downwards, put to it the pickle that was
in the beef when it lay in falt, fet it in a flow
oven all the night, then take it out and bind
it tight, and tie up both ends, the next day
take it out of the cloth, and put it into pickle;
you muft take the fame pickle it was baked
in ; take off the fat and boil the pickle, put
in a handful of falt, a few bay leaves, a little whole Jamaica and black pepper, a quart
of ftale ftrong beer, a little vinegar or alegar ; if you make the pickle very good, it
will keep five or fix months very well ; if
your beef be not too much baked it will cut
all in diamonds.

83. *To roll a* Breast *of* Veal *to eat Cold.*

Take a large breaft of veal, fat and white,
bone it and cut it in two, feafon it with mace;
nutmeg, pepper and falt, on one part you
may ftrinkle a few fweet herbs fhred fine,
roll them tight up, bind them well with coarfe
incle, fo boil it an hour and an half ; you
may make the fame pickle as you did for the
beef, excepting the ftrong beer ; when it is
enough take it up, and bind it as you did
the beef, fo hang it up whilft it be cold.

84. *To*

84. *To pot* Tongues.

Take your tongues and falt them with falt-petre, common falt and bay falt, let them lie ten days, then take them out and boil them whilft they will blanch, cut off the lower part of the tongues, then feafon them with mace, pepper, nutmeg and falt, put them into a pot and fend them to the oven, and the low part of your tongues that you cut off lay up-on your tongue s, and one pound of butter, let them bake whilft they are tender, then take them out of the pot, throw over them a little more feafoning, put them into the pot you defign to keep them in, prefs them down very tight, lay over them a weight, and let them ftand all night, then cover them with clarified butter : You muft not falt your tongues as you do for hanging.

85. *How to pot* Venison.

Take your venifon and cut it in thin pieces, feafon it with pepper and falt, put it into your pot, lay over it fome butter ahd a lit-tle beef-fuit, let it ftand all night in the oven; when it is baked beat it in a mar-ble mortar or wooden bowl, put in part of the gravy, and all the fat you take from it ; when you have beat it put it into your pot, then take the fat lap of a fhoulder of mutton, take off the out-fkin, and roaft it, when it is roafted and cold, cut it in long pieces the thicknefs of your finger ; when you put the venifon into the pot, put it in at three times, betwixt every one lay the mutton crofs your

pot,

pot, at an equal diftance ; if you cut it the right way it will cut all in diamonds ; leave fome of the venifon to lay on the top, and cover it with clarified butter; fo keep it for ufe.

86. *To pot all Sorts of* WILD-FOWL.

When the wild-fowl are dreffed take a pafte-pin, and beat them on the breaft 'till they are flat ; before you roaft them feafon them with mace, nutmeg, pepper and falt ; you mufl not roaft them over much ; when you draw them feafon them on the out-fide, and fet them on one end to drain out the gravy, and put them into your pot ; you may put in two layers ; if you prefs them very flat, cover them with clarified butter when they are cold.

87. *How to pot* BEEF.

Take two pounds of the flice or buttock, feafon it with about two ounces of faltpetre and a little common falt, let it lie two or three days, fend it to the oven, and feafon it with a little pepper, falt and mace ; lay over your beef half a pound of butter or beef fuet, and let it ftand all night in the oven to ftew ; take from it the gravy and the butter, and beat them (with the beef) in a bowl, then take a quarter of a pound of anchovies, bone them, and beat them too with a little of the gravy ; if it be not feafoned enough to your tafte, put to it a little more feafoning ; put it clofe down in a pot, and when it is cold cover it up with butter, and keep it for ufe.

88. *To ragout a* RUMP *of* BEEF.

Take a rump of beef, lard it with bacon
and

and spices, betwixt the larding, stuff it with forc'd meat, made of a pound of veal, three quarters of a pound of beef suit, a quarter of a pound of fat bacon boiled and shred well by itself, a good quantity of parsley, winter savoury, thyme, sweet-marjoram, and an onion, mix all these together, season it with mace cloves, cinamon, salt, Jamaica and black pepper, and some grated bread, work the fore'd meat up with three whites and two yolks of eggs, then stuff it, and lay some rough suet in a stew-pan with your beef upon it, let it fry till it be brown then put in some water, a bunch of sweet herbs, a large onion stuffed with cloves, sliced turnips, carrots cut as large as the yolk of an egg, some whole pepper and salt, half a pint of claret, cover it close, and let it stew fix or seven hours over a gentle fire, turning it very often.

89. *How to make* SAUCE *for it.*

Take truffles, morels, sweet-breads, diced pallets boiled tender, three anchovies, and some lemon-peel, put these into some brown gravy and stew them ; if you do not think it thick enough, dredge in a little flour, and just before you pour it on your beef put in a litttle white wine and vinegar, and serve it up hot.

90. *Sauce for boiled* RABBETS.

Take a few onions, boil them thoroughly, shifting them in water often, mix them well together with a little melted butter and water.

Some

Some add a little pulp of apple and muftard.

91. *To falt a* Leg *of* Mutton *to eat like* Ham.

Take a leg of mutton, an ounce of falt-petre, two ounces of bay falt, rub it in very well, take a quarter of a pound of coarfe fugar, mix it with two or three handfuls of common falt, then take and falt it very well, and let it lie a week, falt it again, and let it lie another week, fo hang it up, and keep it for ufe, after it is dry ufe it, the fooner the better; it won't keep fo long as ham.

92. *How to falt* HAM *or* TONGUES.

Take to a middling ham, two ounces of faltpetre, a quarter of a pound of bay-falt, beat them together, and rub them on your ham very well, before you falt it on the infide, fet your falt before the fire to warm; to every ham take half a pound of coarfe fugar, mix it with a little of the falt, and rub it in very well, let it lie for a week or ten days, then falt it again very well, and let it lie another week or ten days, then hang it to dry, not very near the fire, nor over much in the air.

Take your tongues and clean them, and cut off the root, then take two ounces of faltpetre, a quarter of a pound of bay falt well beaten, three or four tongues, according as they are in bignefs, lay them on a thing by themfelves, for if you lay them under your bacon it flats your tongues, and fpoils them; falt them very well, and let them lie as long as the hams with the fkin-fide downwards: You may do a rump of beef the fame way, only leave out the fugar.

93. *To*

93. *To boil a* Knuckle *of* Veal *with Rice.*

Take a knuckle of veal and a fcrag of mutton, put them into a kettle with as much water as will cover them, and half a pound of rice; before you put in the rice let the kettle be fkim'd very well, it will make the rice the whiter; put in a blade or two of mace, and a little falt, fo let them boil all together till the rice and meat be thoroughly enough; you muft not let the broth be over thick; ferve it up with the knuckle in the middle of the difh and fippets round it.

94. *To ftew* Ducks *whole.*

Take ducks when they are drawn and clean wafh'd, put them into a ftew-pan with ftrong broth, claret, mace, whole pepper, an onion, an anchovy and lemon-peel; when well ftewed put in a piece of butter and fome grated bread to thicken it; lay round them crifp bacon and forc'd-meat balls. Garnifh with fhalots.

95. *To pot a* Hare.

Take a hare, cafe, wafh, and wipe her dry, cut her in pieces, keep out all the bloody parts and fkins, feafon it with mace, pepper and falt, put it into a pot, and lay over it a pound of beef-fuet, let it ftand all night in a flow oven; when it is baked take out all the bones, and chop it all together in a bowl with the fat and gravy that comes from it, put it tight down into a pot, and when cold cover it with clarified butter: If you have no diflike to

bacon

bacon, you may put in two or three slices when you send it to the oven.

96. *How to make a* HARE-PIE.

Parboil the hare, take out all the bones, and beat the meat in a mortar with some fat pork or new bacon, then soak it in claret all night, the next day take it out, season it with pepper, salt and nutmeg, then lay the back bone into the middle of the pie, put the meat about it with about three quarters of a pound of butter, and bake it in puff-paste, but lay no paste in the bottom of the dish.

97. *To make a* HARE-PIE *another way.*

Take the flesh of a hare after it is skined, and string it: take a pound of beef-suet or marrow shred small, with sweet-marjoram, parsley and shalots, take the hare, cut it in pieces, season it with mace, pepper, salt and nutmeg, then bake it either in cold or hot paste, and when it is baked open it and put to it some melted butter.

98. *To make* PIG *Royal.*

Take a pig and roast it the same way as you did for lamb, when you draw it you must not cut it up; when it is cold you must lard it with bacon; cut not your layers too small, if you do they will melt away, cut them about an inch and a quarter long; you must put one row down the back, and one on either side, then strinkle it over with a few bread-crumbs and a little salt, and set it in the oven, an hour will bake it, but mind your oven be not too hot; you must take another pig of a

less

lefs fize, roaft it, cut it up, and lie it on each
fide : The fauce you make for a roaft pig
will ferve for both.

This is proper for a bottom difb at a grand
entertainment.

99. *To roaft* VEAL *a favoury way.*

When you have ftuffed your veal, ftrew
fome of the ingredients over it ; when it is
roafted make your fauce of what drops from
the meat, put an anchovy in water, and
when diffolved pour it into the dripping-pan,
with a large lump of butter and oyfters ;
tofs it up with flour to thicken it.

100. *To make a* HAM PIE.

Cut the ham round, and lay it in water all
night, boil it tender as you would do for eating, take off the fkin, ftrew over it a little
pepper, and bake it in a deep difh, put to it
a pint of water, and half a pound of butter ;
you muft bake it in puff-palte ; but lay no
pafte in the bottom of the difh ; when you
fend it to the table fend it without a lid.

It is proper for a top or bottom difh either
fummer or winter.

101. *To make a* NEAT'S TONGUE PIE.

Take two or three tongues, (according as
you would have your pie in bignefs) cut off
the roots and low parts, take two ounces of
falt-petre, a little bay falt, rub them very well,
lay them on an earthen difb with the fkin fide
downwards, let them lie for a week or ten
days, whilft they be very red, then boil them
as tender as you would have them for eating,
blanch

blanch and feafon with a little pepper and falt, flat them as much as you can, bake them in puff pafte in a deep difh, but lay no pafte in the bottom, put to them a little gravy, and half a pound of butter; lay your tongues with the wrong fide upwards, when they are baked turn them, and ferve it up without a lid.

102. To broil SHEEP or HOG's TONGUES.

Boil, blanch, and fplit your tongues, feafon them with a little pepper and falt, then dip them in egg, ftrew over them a few bread-crumbs, and broil them whilft they be brown; ferve them up with a little gravy and butter.

103. To Pickle PORK.

Cut off the leg, fhoulder pieces, the bloody neck and the fpare-rib as bare as you can, then cut the middle pieces as large as they can lie in the tub, falt them with faltpetre, bay-falt, and white falt; your faltpetre muft be beat fmall, and mix'd with the other falts; half a peck of white falt, a quart of bay-falt, and half a pound of faltpetre, is enough for a large hog; you muft rub the pork very well with your falt, then lay a thick layer of falt all over the tub, then a piece of pork, and do fo till all your pork is in; lay the fkin fide downwards, fill up all the hollows and fides of the tub with little pieces that are not bloody, prefs all down as clofe as poffible, and lay on a good layer of falt on the top, then lay on the legs and fhoulder pieces, which muft be ufed firft, the reft will keep two years if not

C
pulled

pulled up, nor the pickle poured from it. You muſt obſerve to ſee it be covered with pickle.

104. *To fricaſſee* CALF'S FEET *white*.

Dreſs the calf's feet, boil them as you would do for eating, take out the long bones, cut them in two, and put them into a ſtew-pan with a little white gravy, and a ſpoonful or two of white wine ; take the yolks of two or three eggs, two or three ſpoonfuls of cream, grate in a little nutmeg and ſalt, and ſhake all together with a lump of butter. Garniſh your diſh with ſlices of lemon and currants, and ſo ſerve them up.

105. *To roll a* PIG's *Head to eat like Brawn.*

Take a large pig's head, cut off the groin ends, crack the bones and put it in water, ſhift it once or twice, cut off the ears, then boil it ſo tender that the bones will ſlip out, nick it with a knife in the thick part of the head, throw over it a pretty large handful of ſalt ; take half a dozen of large neat's feet, boil them while they be ſoft, ſplit them, and take out all the bones and black bits ; take a ſtrong coarſe cloth, and lay the feet with the ſkin ſide downwards, with all the looſe pieces on the inſide ; preſs them with your hand to make them of an equal thickneſs, lay them at that length that they will reach round the head, and throw over them a handful of ſalt, then lay the head acroſs, one thick part one way, and the other another, that the fat may appear alike at both ends ; leave one

foot

foot out to lay at the top to make a lantern to reach round, bind it with filleting as
your would do brawn, and tie it very clofe at
both ends ; you may take it out of the cloth
the next day, take off the filleting and wafh
it, wrap it about again very tight, and keep
it in brawn-pickle.

This has been often taken for real brawn.

106. *How to fry* CALF's FEET *in Butter*.

Take four calf's feet and blanch them, boil
them as you would do for eating, take out
the large bones and cut them in two, beat a
fpoonful of wheat flour and four eggs together, put to it a little nutmeg, pepper and
falt, dip in your calf's feet, and fry them
in butter a light brown, and lay them upon
your difh with a little melted butter over
them. Garnifh with flices of lemon and
ferve them up.

107. *How to make* SAVOURY PATTEES.

Take the kidney of a loyn of veal before
it be roafted, cut it in thin flices, feafon it
with mace, pepper and falt, and make your
pattees ; lay in every patty a flice, and either
bake or fry them.

You may make marrow pattees the fame way.

108. *To make* EGG PIES.

Take and boil half a dozen eggs, half a
dozen apples, a pound and a half of beef-
fuet, a pound of currants, and fhred them,
fo feafon it with mace, nutmeg and fugar to
your tafte, a fpoonful or two of brandy; and
fweet meats, if you pleafe.

109. *To*

109. *To make a sweet* CHICKEN PIE.

Break the chicken bones, cut them in little
bits, season them lightly with mace and salt,
take the yolks of four eggs boiled hard ahd
quartered, five artichoke - bottoms, half a
pound of raisins of the sun, stoned, half a pound
of citron, half a pound of lemon, half a pound
of marrow, a few forc'd-meat balls, and half
a pound of currans well cleaned, so make a
light puff-paste, but put no paste in the bottom ; when it is baked take a little white wine,
a little juice of either orange or lemon, the
yolk of an egg well beat, and mix them together, make it hot and put it into your pie ;
when you serve it up take the same ingredients
you use for a lamb or veal pie, only leave out
the artichokes.

110. *To roast* TONGUES.

Cut off the roots of two tongues, take
three ounces of saltpetre, a little bay-salt and
common salt, rub them very well, let them
lie a week or ten days to make them red,
but not salt, so boil them tender as they will
blanch, strew over them a few bread-crumbs,
set them before the fire to brown, and turn
them to make them brown on every side.

To make SAUCE *for the* TONGUES.

Take a few bread crumbs, and as much
water as will wet them, then put in claret
till they be red, and a little beat cinnamon,
sweeten it to your taste, put a little gravy on
the dish with your tongues, and the sweet

sauc

sauce in two basons, set them on each side, so serve them up.

111. *To fry* CALF's FEET *in Eggs.*

Boil your calf's feet as you would do for eating, take out the long bones and split them in two, when they are cold season 'em with a little pepper, salt and m g; take three eggs, put to them a spoonful of flour, so, dip the feet in it and fry them in butter; you must have a little gravy and butter for sauce. Garnish with currans, so serve them up.

112. *To make a* MINC'D PIE *of Calf's Feet.*

Take two or three calf's feet, and boil them as you would do for eating, take out the long bones, shred them very fine, put to them double their weight of beef-suet shred fine, and about a pound of currans well cleaned, a quarter of a pound of candid orange and citron cut in small pieces, half a pound of sugar, a little salt, a quarter of an ounce of mace and a large nutmeg, beat them together, put in a little juice of lemon or verjuice to your taste, a glass of mountain wine or sack, which you please, so mix all together; bake them in puff-paste.

113. *To roast a* WOODCOCK.

When you have dress'd your woodcock, and drawn it under the leg, take out the bitter bit, put in the train again; whilst the woodcock is roasting set under it an earthen dish with either water in or small gravy, let the woodcock drop into it, take the gravy

and

and put to it a little butter, and thicken it with
flour ; your woodcock will take about ten
minutes roasting if you have a brisk fire ;
when you dish it up lay round it wheat bread
toasts, and pour the sauce over the toasts,
and serve it up.

You may roast a partridge the same way,
only add crumb sauce in a bason.

114. *To make a* CALF's HEAD PIE.

Take a calf's head and clean it, boil it as
you would do for hasbing, when it is cold cut
it in thin slices, and season it with a little black
pepper, nutmeg, salt, a few shred capers, a
few oysters and cockles, two or three mushrooms, and green lemon peel, mix them all
well together, put them into your pie ; it must
not be a standing pie, but baked in a flat
pewter dish, with a rim of puff paste round
the edge ; when you have filled the pie with
the meat, lay on forc'd-meat balls, and the
yolks of some hard eggs, put in a little small
gravy and butter ; when it comes from the
oven take off the lid, put into it a little white
wine to your taste, and shake up the pie, so
serve it up without lid.

115. *To make a* CALF's FOOT PIE.

Take two or three calf's feet, according
as you would have your pie in bigness, boil
and bone them as you would do for eating,
and when cold cut them in thin slices ; take
about three quarters of a pound of beef-suet
shred fine, half a pound of raisins stoned, half
a pound of cleaned currants, a little mace and
nut-

meg, green lemon-peel, falt, fugar, and candid lemon or orange, mix altogether, and put them into a difh, make a good puff-pafte, but let there be no pafte in the bottom of the difb ; when it is baked, take off the lid, and fqueeze in a little lemon or verjuice, cut the lid in fippets and lay round.

116. *To make a* WOODCOCK PIE.

Take three or four brace of woodcocks, according as you would have the pie in big-nefs, drefs and fkewer them as you would do for roafting, draw them, and feafon the in-fide with a little pepper, falt and mace, but don't wafh them, put the train into the belly again, but nothing elfe, for there is fome-thing in them that gives them a bitterer tafte in the baking than in the roafting, when you put them into the difh lay them with the breaft downwards, beat them upon the breaft as flat as you can ; you muft feafon them on the outfide as you do the infide ; bake them in puff-pafte, but lay none in the bottom of the difh, put to them a jill of gravy and a little butter ; you muft be very careful your pie be not too much baked ; when you ferve it up take off the lid and turn the woodcocks with the breaft upwards.

You may bake partridge the fame way.

117. *To pickle* PIGEONS.

Take your pigeons and bone them ; you muft begin to bone them at the neck and turn the fkin downwards, when they are boned feafon them with pepper, falt and nutmeg;

C 4

few

few up both ends, and boil them in water and white wine vinegar, a few bay leaves, a little whole pepper and falt; when they are enough take them out of the pickle, and boil it down with a little more falt; when it is cold put in the pigeons and keep them for ufe.

118. *To make a fweet* VEAL PIE.

Take a loin of veal, cut off the thin part length ways, cut the reft in thin flices, as much as you have occafion for, flat it with your bill, and cut off the bone ends next the chine, feafon it with nutmeg and falt; take half a pound of raifins ftoned, and half a pound of currans well clean'd, mix all toge-ther, and lay a few of them at the bottom of the difh, lay a layer of meat; and betwixt every layer lay on your fruit, but leave fome for the top; you muft make a puff-pafte, but lay none in the bottom of the difb; when you have filled your pie, put in a jill of water and a little butter, when it is baked, have a caudle to put into it.

To make the caudle, fee receipt 177.

119. MINC'D PIES *another way.*

Take a pound of the fineft feam tripes you can get, a pound and a half of beef fuet, and chop them very fine; a pound and a half of currans well cleaned, two, three or four ap-ples pared and fhred very fine, a little green lemon-peel and mace fbred, a large nutmeg, a glafs of fack or brandy, (which you pleafe) half a pound of fugar, and a little falt, fo mix them well together, and fill your petty-pans, then

then ftick five or fix bits of candid lemon or orange in every petty-pan, cover them, and when baked they are fit for ufe.

120. *To make a favoury* CHICKEN PIE.

Take half a dozen fmall chickens, feafon them with mace, pepper and falt, both in-fide and out ; then take three or four veal fweet-breads, feafon them with the fame, and lay round them a few forc'd-meat balls, put in a little water and butter ; take a little white gravy not over ftrong, fnted a few oyfters if you have any, and a little lemon-peel, fqueeze in a little lemon juice, not to make it four ; if you have no oyfters take the whiteft of your fweet-breads and boil them, cut them fmall, and put them into your gravy, thicken it with a little butter and flour ; when you open the pie, if there be any fat, fkim it off, and pour the fauce over the chick-ens breafts ; fo ferve it up without lid.

121. *To roaft a* HANCH *of* VENISON.

Take a hanch of venifon and fpit it, then take a little bread meal, knead and roll it very thin, lay it over the fat part of your venifon with a paper over it, tye it round your veni-fon with a pack-thread; if it be a large hanch it will take four hours roafting, and a mid-dling hanch three hours ; keep it bafting all the time you roaft it ; when you difh it up put a little gravy in the difb, and fweet fauce in a bafon ; half an hour before you draw your venifon take off the pafte, bafte it, and let it be a light brown.

C 5

122. *To make* SWEET PATTEES.

Take the kidney of a loyn of veal with the fat, when roasted shred it very fine, put to it a little shred mace, nutmeg and salt, about half a pound of currants, the juice of a lemon, and sugar to your taste, then bake them in puff-paste ; you may either fry or bake them.

They are proper for a side-dish.

123. *To make* BEEF-ROLLS.

Cut your beef thin as for scotch collops, beat it very well, and season it with salt, Jamaica and white pepper, mace, nutmeg, sweet marjoram, parsley, thyme, and a little onion shred small, rub them on the collops on one side, then take long bits of beef suet and roll in them, tying them up with a thread ; flour them well, and fry them in butter very brown ; then have ready some good gravy and stew them an hour and a half, stirring them often, and keep them covered, when they are enough take off the threads, and put in a little flour, with a good lump of butter, and squeeze in some lemon, then they are ready for use.

124. *To make a* HERRING-PIE *of* WHITE SALT HERRINGS.

Take five or six salt herrings, wash them very well, lay them in a pretty quantity of water all night to take out the saltness, season them with a little black pepper, three or four middling onions peel'd and shred very fine, lay one part of them at the bottom of the pie,

and

and the other at the top ; to five or fix herrings put in half a pound of butter, then lay
in your herrings whole, only take off the
heads ; make them into a ftanding pie with
a thin cruft.

125. *How to Collar* PIG.

Take a large pig that is fat, about a month
old, kill and drefs it, cut off the head, cut it
in two down the back and bone it, then cut it
in three or four pieces, wafh it in a little water
to take out the blood : take a little milk and
water juft warm, put in your pig, let it lie
about a day and a night, fhift it two or three
times in that time to make it white, then take
it out and wipe it very well with a dry cloth,
and feafon it with mace, nutmeg, pepper and
falt ; take a little fhred parfley and ftrinkle it
over two of the quarters, fo roll them up in a
fine foft cloth, tie it up at both ends, bind
it tight with a little filleting or coarfe incle,
and boil it in milk and water with a little falt ;
it will take about an hour and a half boiling ;
when it is enough bind it up tight in your
cloth again, and hang it up whilft it be cold.
For the pickle boil a little milk and water, a
few bay leaves and a little falt ; when it is
cold take your pig out of the cloths and put
it into the pickle ; you muft fhift it out of
your pickle two or three times to make it
white, the laft pickle make ftrong, and put
in a little whole pepper, a pretty large handful of falt, a few bay leaves, and fo keep
it for ufe.

126. *To Collar* SALMON.

Take the fide of a middling falmon, and cut off the head, take out all the bones and the outfide, feafon it with mace, nutmeg, pepper and falt, roll it tight up in a cloth, boil it, and bind it up with incle ; it will take about an hour boiling ; when it is boiled bind it tight again, when cold take it very carefully out of the cloth and bind it about with filleting ; you muft not take off the filleting but as it is eaten.

To make PICKLE *to keep it in.*

Take two or three quarts of water, a jill of vinegar, a little Jamaica pepper and whole pepper, a large handful of falt, boil them altogether, and when it is cold put in your falmon, fo keep it for ufe : If your pickle don't keep, you muft renew it.

You may collar pike the fame way.

127. *To make an* OYSTER PIE.

Take a pint of the largeft oyfters you can get, clean them very well in their own liquor, if you have not liquor enough, add to them three or four fpoonfuls of water ; take the kidney of a loin of veal, cut it in thin flices, and feafon it with a little pepper and falt, lay the flices in the bottom of the difh, (but there muft be no pafte in the bottom of the difh) cover them with the oyfters, ftrew over a little of the feafoning as you did for the veal ; take the marrow of one or two bones, lay it over your oyfters and cover them with puff-pafte ; when it is baked take off the lid, put into it

a fpoonful

a ſpoonful or two of white wine, ſhake it up
altogether, and ſerve it up.

It is proper for a ſide-diſh, either for noon
or night.

128. *To butter* CRAB *and* LOBSTER.

Dreſs all the meat out of the belly and claws
of your lobſter, put it into a ſtew-pan, with
two or three ſpoonfuls of water, a ſpoonful
or two of white wine vinegar, a little pepper,
ſhred mace, and a lump of butter, ſhake it
over the ſtove till it be very hot, but do not
let it boil, if you do it will oil ; put it into
your diſh, and lay round it your ſmall claws :
It is as proper to put it in ſcallop ſhells as on
a diſh.

129. *To roaſt a* LOBSTER.

If your lobſter be alive tie it to the ſpit,
roaſt and baſte it for half an hour ; if it be
boiled you muſt put it in boiling water, and
let it have one boil, then lie it in a dripping-
pan and baſte it ; when you lay it upon the
diſh, ſplit the tail, and lay it on each ſide, ſo
ſerve it up with a little melted butter in a
china cup.

130. *To make a* QUAKING PUDDING.

Take eight eggs and beat them very well,
put to them three ſpoonfuls of London flour,
a little ſalt, three jills of cream, and boil it
with a ſtick of cinnamon and a blade of mace;
when it is cold mix it to your eggs and flour,
butter your cloth, and do not give it over
much room in your cloth ; about half an hour
will boil it ; you muſt turn it in the boiling

or

or the flour will settle, so serve it up with a
little melted butter.

131. *A* HUNTING PUDDING.

Take a pound of fine flour, a pound of
beef suet shred fine, three quarters of a pound
of currants well cleaned, a quartern of raisins
stoned and shred, five eggs, a little lemon-
peel shred fine, half a nutmeg grated, a jill
of cream, a little salt, about two spoonfuls
of sugar, and a little brandy, so mix all well
together, and tie it up tight in your cloth ;
it will take two hours boiling ; you must have
a little white wine and butter for your sauce.

132. *A* CALF's-FOOT PUDDING.

Take two calf's-feet, when they are clean'd
boil them as you would for eating ; take out
all the bones ; when they are cold shred them
in a wooden bowl as small as bread crumbs ;
then take the crumbs of a penny loaf, three
quarters of a pound of beef suet shred fine,
grate in half a nutmeg, take half a pound of
currants well washed, half a pound of raisins
stoned and shred, half a pound of sugar, six
eggs, and a little salt, mix them all together
very well, with as much cream as will wet
them, so butter your cloth and tie it up tight;
it will take two hours boiling ; you may if
you please stick it with a little orange, and
serve it up.

133. *A* SAGOO PUDDING.

Take three or four ounces of sagoo, and
wash it in two or three waters, set it on to
boil

boil in a pint of water, when you think it is enough take it up, fet it to cool, and take half of a candid lemon fhred fine, grate in half of a nutmeg, mix two ounces of Jordan almonds blanched, grate in three ounces of bifcuit if you have it, if not a few bread crumbs grated, a little rofe-water and half a pint of cream ; then take fix eggs, leave out two of the whites, beat them with a fpoonful or two of fack, put them to your fagoo, with about half a pound of clarified butter, mix them all together, then fweeten it with fine fugar, put in a little falt, and bake it in a difh with a little puff-pafte about the difh edge, when you ferve it up you may ftick a little citron or candid orange, or any fweet-meats you pleafe.

134. A Marrow Pudding.

Take a penny loaf, take off the outfide, then cut one half in thin flices ; take the marrow of two bones, half a pound of currants well cleaned, fhred your marrow, and ftrinkle a little marrow and currants over the difh ; lay over it your bread, in thin flices, whilft you fill the difh ; if you have not marrow enough you may add to it a little beef fuet fhred fine ; take five eggs and beat them very well, put to them three jills of milk, grate in half a nutmeg, fweeten it to your tafte, mix all together, pour it over your pudding, and fave a little marrow to ftrinkle over the top of your pudding ; when you fend it to the oven lye a puff-pafte round the difh edge.

135. A Car-

135. *A* Carrot Pudding.

Take three or four clear red carrots, boil and peel them, take the red part of the carrot, beat it very fine in a marble mortar, put to it the crumbs of a penny loaf, fix eggs, half a pound of clarified butter, two or three fpoonfuls of rofe-water, a little lemon-peel fhred, grate in a little nutmeg, mix them well together, bake it with a puff-pafte round your difh, and have a little white wine, butter and fugar, for the fauce.

136. *A* Ground Rice Pudding.

Take half a pound of ground rice, half cree it in a quart of milk, when it is cold put to it five eggs well beat, a jill of cream, a little lemon-peel fhred fine, half a nutmeg grated, half a pound of butter, and half a pound of fugar, mix them well together, put them into your difh with a little falt, and bake it with a puff-pafte round your difh ; have a little rofe-water, butter and fugar to pour over it : You may prick in it candid lemon or citron if you pleafe.

Half of the above quantity will make a pudding for a fide-difh.

137. *A* Potatoe Pudding.

Take three or four large potatoes, boil them as you would do for eating, beat them with a little rofe-water and a glafs of fack in a marble mortar, put to them half a pound of fugar, fix eggs, half a pound of melted butter, half a pound of currans well cleaned, a
little

little fhred lemon-peel, and candid orange, mix altogether and ferve it up.

138. *An* APPLE PUDDING.

Take half a dozen large codlins, or pippins, roaft them and take out the pulp; take eight eggs, (leave out fix of the whites) half a pound of fine powder fugar, beat your eggs and fugar well together, and put to them the pulp of your apples, half a pound of clarified butter, a little lemon-peel fhred fine, a handful of bread crumbs or bifcuit, four ounces of candid orange or citron, and bake it with a thin pafte under it.

139. *An* ORANGE PUDDING.

Take three large feville oranges, the cleareft kind you can get, grate off all the outrhine; take eight eggs, (leave out fix of the whites) half a pound of double refined fugar, beat and put it to your eggs, then beat them both together for half an hour; take three ounces of fweet almonds blanch'd, beat them with a fpoonful or two of fair water to keep them from oiling, half a pound of butter, melt it without water, and the juice of two oranges, then put in the rafpings of your oranges, and mix all together; lay a thin pafte over your difh and bake it, but not in too hot an oven.

140. *An* ORANGE PUDDING *another Way*.

Take half a pound of candid orange, cut them in thin flices, and beat them in a marble mortar to a pulp; take fix eggs, (leave out half of the whites) half a pound of but-

ter

ter, and the juice of one orange ; mix them together, and fweeten it with fine powder fugar, then bake it with thin pafte under it.

141. *An* ORANGE PUDDING *another Way.*

Take three or four feville oranges, the cleareft fkins you can get, pare them very thin, boil the peel in a pretty quantity of water, fhift them two or three times in the boiling to take out the bitter tafte ; when it is boiled you muft beat it very fine in a marble mortar; take ten eggs, (leave out fix of the whites) three-quarters of a pound of loaf fugar, beat it and put it to your eggs, beat them together for half an hour, put to them half a pound of melted butter, and the juice of two or three oranges, as they are of goodnefs, mix all together, and bake it with a thin pafte over your difh.

This will make cheefe-cakes as well as a pudding.

142. *An* ORANGE PUDDING *another Way.*

Take five or fix feville oranges, grate them and make a hole in the top, take out all the meat, and boil the fkins very tender, fhifting them in the boiling to take off the bitter tafte; take half a pound of long bifcuit, flice and fcald them with a little cream, beat fix eggs and put to your bifcuit ; take half a pound of currants, wafh them clean, grate in half a nutmeg, put in a little falt and a glafs of fack, beat all together, then put it into your orange fkins ; tie them tight in a piece of fine cloth, every one feparate ; about three

quarters

quarters of an hour will boil them. You muſt have a little white wine, butter and ſugar for ſauce.

143. *To make an* ORANGE PIE.

Take half a dozen ſeville oranges, chip them very fine as you would do for preſerving, make a little hole in the top, and ſcope out all the meat, as you would do an apple, you muſt boil them whilſt they are tender, and ſhift them two or-three times to take off the bitter taſte; take fix or eight apples, according as they are in bigneſs, pare and ſlice them, and put to them part of the pulp of your oranges, and pick out the ſtrings and pippins, put to them half a pound of fine powder ſugar, ſo boil it up over a ſlow fire, as you would do for puffs, and fill your oranges with it; they muſt be baked in a deep delf diſh with no paſte under them; when you put them into your diſh put under them three quarters of a pound of fine powder ſugar, put in as much water as will wet your ſugar, and put your oranges with the open ſide uppermoſt; it will take about an hour and half baking in a ſlow oven; lie over them a light puff-paſte; when you diſh it up take off the lid, and turn the oranges in the pie, cut the lid in ſippets, and ſet them at equal diſtances, ſo ſerve it up.

144. *To make a quaking* PUDDING *another way.*

Take a pint of cream, boil it with one ſtick of cinnamon, take out the ſpice when it is boiled, then take the yolks of eight eggs, and

four

four whites, beat them very well with fome
fack, and mix your eggs with the cream, a
little fugar and falt, half a penny wheat loaf,
a fpoonful of flour, a quarter of a pound of
almonds blanch'd and beat fine, beat them
altogether, wet a thick cloth, flour it, and
put it in when the pot boils; it muft boil an
hour at leaft: melted butter, fack and fugar
is fauce for it; ftick blanch'd almonds and
candid orange-peel on the top, fo ferve it up.

145. *To make* PLUMB PORRIDGE.

Take two fhanks of beef, and ten quarts
of water, let it boil over a flow fire till it be
tender, and when the broth is ftrong, ftrain it
out, wipe the pot and put in the broth again,
flice in two penny loaves thin, cutting off the
top and bottom, put fome of the liquor to
it, cover it up and let it ftand for a quarter of
an hour, fo put it into the pot again, and let
it boil a quarter of an hour, then put in
four pounds of currans, and let them boil a
little; then put in two pounds of raifins, and
two pounds of prunes, let them boil till they
fwell; then put in a quarter of an ounce of
mace, a few cloves beat fine, mix it with a
little water, and put it into your pot; alfo a
pound of fugar, a little falt, a quart or better of claret, and the juice of two or three
lemons or verjuice; thicken it with fagoo
inftead of bread; fo put it in earthen pots,
and keep it for ufe.

146. *To make a* PALPATOON *of* PIGEONS.

Take mufhrooms, pallets, oyfters and
fweet-

sweet-breads, fry them in butter, put all these
in a strong gravy, heat them over the fire,
and thicken them up with an egg and a little
butter; then take six or eight pigeons, truss
them as you would for baking, season them
with pepper and salt, and lay on them a crust
of forc'd meat as follows, *viz.* a pound of
veal cut in little bits, and a pound and a half
of marrow, beat it together in a stone mortar, after it is beat very fine, season it with
mace, pepper and salt, put in the yolks of
four eggs, and two raw eggs, mix altogether with a few bread crumbs to a paste:
make the sides and lid of your pie with it,
then put your ragout into your dish, and lay
in your pigeons with butter; an hour and a
half will bake it.

147. *To fry* Cucumbers *for Mutton Sauce.*

You must brown some butter in a pan, and
cut six middling cucumbers, pare and slice
them, but not over thin, drain them from the
water, then put them into the pan, when
they are fried brown put to them a little pepper and salt, a lump of butter, a spoonful
of vinegar, a little shred onion, and a little
gravy, not to make it too thin, so shake them
well together with a little flour.

You may lay them round your mutton, or
they are proper for a side-dish.

148. *To force a* Fowl.

Take a good fowl, pull and draw it, then
flit the skin down the back, take the flesh
from the bones, and mince it very well, mix
it

it with a little beef-fuer, fhred a jill of large
oyfters, chóp a fhalot, a little grated bread,
and fome fweet herbs, mix all together, feafon it with nutmeg, pepper and falt, make
it up with yolks of eggs, put it on the bones
and draw the fkin over it, few up the back,
cut off, the legs, and put the bones as you
do a fowl for boiling, tie the fowl up in a
cloth ; an hour will boil it. For fauce take
a few oyfters, fhred them, and put them into a little gravy, with a lump of butter, a
little lemon peel fhred and a little juice,
thicken it up with a little flour, lie the
fowl on the difh, and pour the fauce upon
it ; you may fry a little of the forc'd meat to
lay round. Garnifh your difh with lemon ;
you may fet it in the oven if you have convenience, only rub over it the yolk of an egg
and a few bread crumbs.

149. *To make* STRAWBERRY *and* RASBERRY
FOOL.

Take a pint of rafberries, fqueeze and ftrain
the juice, with a fpoonful of orange water,
put to the juice fix ounces of fine fugar, and
boil it over the fire ; then take a pint of
cream and boil it, mix them all well together,
and heat them over the fire, but not to boil,
if it do it will curdle ; ftir it till it be cold,
put it into your bafon and keep it for ufe.

150. *To make a* POSSET *with* Almonds.

Blanch and beat three quarters of a pound
of almonds, fo fine that they will fpread betwixt your fingers like butter, put in water

as

as you beat them to keep them from oiling; take a pint of fack, cherry or goofeberry wine, and fweeten it to your tafte with double refin'd fugar, make it boiling hot; take the almonds, put to them a little water, and boil the wine and almonds together; take the yolks of four eggs, and beat them very well, put to them three or four fpoonfuls of wine, then put it into your pan by degrees, ftirring it all the while; when it begins to thicken take it off, and ftir it a little, put it into a china dilh, and ferve it up.

151. To make DUTCH-BEEF.

Take the lean part of a buttock of beef raw, rub it well with brown fugar all over, and let it lie in a pan or tray two or three hours, turning it three or four times, then falt it with common falt, and two ounces of faltpetre; let it lie a fortnight, turning it every day, then roll it very ftraight, and put it into a cheefe prefs a day and night, then take off the cloth and hang it up to dry in the chimney; when you boil it let it be boiled very well, it will cut in fhivers like dutch beef.

You may do a leg of mutton the fame way.

152. To make BOLOGNA SAUSAGES.

Take part of a leg of pork or veal, pick it clean from the fkin or fat, put to every pound of lean meat a pound of beef-fuet pick'd from the fkins, fbred the meat and fuet feparate and very fine, mix them well together, add a large handful of green fage fbred very fmall; feafon it with pepper and falt, mix it well

well, prefs it down hard in an earthen pot, and keep it for ufe.——When you ufe them roll them up with as much egg as will make them roll fmooth ; in rolling them up make them about the length of your fingers, and as thick as two fingers ; fry them in butter, which muft be boiled hot before you put them in, and keep them rolling about in the pan ; when they are fried through they are enough.

153. *To make an* AMBLET *of* COCKLES.

Take four whites and two yolks of eggs, a pint of cream, a little flour, a nutmeg· grated, a little falt, and a jill of cockles, mix all together, and fry it brown.

This is proper for a fide-difh either for noon or night.

154. *To make a common quaking* PUDDING.

Take five eggs, beat them well with a lit- tle falt, put in three fpoonfuls of fine flour, take a pint of new milk and beat them well together, then take a cloth, butter and flour it, but do not give it over much room in the cloth ; an hour will boil it, give it a turn every now and then at the firft putting in, or elfe the meal will fettle to the bottom ; have a little plain butter for fauce, and ferve it up.

155. *To make a boiled* TANSEY.

Take an old penny loaf, cut off the out cruft, flice it thin, put to it as much hot cream as will wet it, fix eggs well beaten, a little fhred lemon-peel, grate in a little nutmeg, and a little falt ; green it as you did your baked
tanfey,

tanfey, fo tie it up in a cloth and boil it;
it will take an hour and a quarter boiling;
when you difh it up ftick it with candid orange
and lay a feville orange cut in quarters round
the difh; ferve it up with melted butter.

156. *A* Tansey *another Way.*

Take an old penny loaf, cut off the out
cruft, flice it very thin, and put to it as much
hot milk as will wet it; take fix eggs, beat
them very well, grate in half a nutmeg, a little fhred lemon-peel, half a pound of clarified butter, half a pound of fugar, and a little
falt; mix them well together. *To green your
Tanfey,* Take a handful or two of fpinage, a
handful of tanfey, and a handful of forrel,
clean them and beat them in a marble mortar,
or grind them as you would do greenfauce,
ftrain them through a linen cloth into a bafon,
and put into your tanfey as much of the juice
as will green it, pour over for the fauce a little white wine, butter and fugar; lay a rim
of pafte round your difh and bake it; when
you ferve it up cut a feville orange in quarters, and lay it round the edge of the difh.

157. *To make* Rice Pancakes.

Take half a pound of rice, wafh and pick
it clean, cree it in fair water till it be a jelly,
when it is cold take a pint of cream and the
yolks of four eggs, beat them very well together, and put them to the rice, with grated
nutmeg and fome falt, then put in half a
pound of butter, and as much flour as will
make it thick enough to fry, with as little
butter as you can.   D   158 *To*

158. *To make* FRUIT FRITTERS.

Take a penny loaf, cut off the out cruft, flice it, put to it as much hot milk as will wet it, beat five or fix eggs, put to them a quarter of a pound of currants, well cleaned, and a little candid orange fbred fine, fo mix them well together, drop them with a fpoon into a ftew-pan in clarified butter ; have a little white wine, butter and fugar for your fauce, put it into a china bafon, lay your fritters round, grate a little fugar over them, and ferve them up.

159. *To make* WHITE PUDDINGS *in fkins.*

Take half a pound of rice, cree it in milk while it be foft, when it is creed put it into a colander to drain ; take a penny loaf, cut off the out cruft, then cut it in thin flices. fcald it in a little milk, but do not make it over wet ; take fix eggs and beat them very well, a pound of currants well cleaned, a pound of beef-fuet fbred fine, two or three fpoonfuls of rofe-water, half a pound of powder fugar, a little falt, a quarter of an ounce of mace, a large nutmeg grated, and a fmall ftick of cinnamon ; beat them toge-ther, mix them very well, and put them into the fkins ; if you find it be too thick put to it a little cream ; you may boil them near half an hour, it will make them keep the better.

160. *To make* BLACK PUDDINGS.

Take two quarts of whole oatmeal, pick it and half boil it, give it room in your cloth,

(you

(you muſt do it the day before you uſe it)
put it into the blood while it is warm, with a
handful of ſalt, ſtir it very well, beat eight
or nine eggs in about a pint of cream, and
a quart of bread-crumbs, a handful or two
of meſlin meal dreſs'd through a hair-ſieve,
if you have it, if not put in wheat flour ; to
this quantity you may put an ounce of Jamaica pepper, an ounce of black pepper, a
large nutmeg, and a little more ſalt, ſweet-
marjoram and thyme, if they be green ſbred
them fine, if dry rub them to powder, mix
them well together, and if it be too thick put
to it a little milk ; take four pounds of beef-
ſuer, and four pounds of lard, ſkin and cut
it in thin pieces, put it into your blood by
handfuls, as you fill your puddings ; when
they are filled and tied prick them with a
pin, it will keep them from burſting in the
boiling ; (you muſt boil them twice) cover
them cloſe and it will make them black.

161. *An* ORANGE PUDDING *another Way.*

Take two ſeville oranges, the largeſt and
cleareſt you can get, grate off the outer ſkin
with a clean grater ; take eight eggs, (leave
out two of the whites) half a pound of loaf
ſugar, beat it very fine, put it to your eggs,
and beat them for an hour, put to them
half a pound of clarified butter, and four
ounces of almonds blanch'd, and beat them
with a little roſe-water ; put in the juice of
the oranges, but mind you don't put in the
pippins, and mix altogether ; bake it with a

thin

thin pafte over the bottom of the difh. It
muft be baked in a flow oven.

162. *To make* APPLE FRITTERS.

Take four eggs and beat them very well,
put to them four fpoonfuls of fine flour, a
little milk, about a quarter of a pound of fugar, a little nutmeg and falt, fo beat them
very well together ; you muft not make it
very thin, if you do it will not ftick to the
apple ; take a middling apple and pare it,
cut out the core, and cut the reft in round
flices about the thicknefs of a fhilling ; (you
may take out the core after you have cut it
with your thimble) have ready a little lard
in a ftew-pan, or any other deep pan ; then
take your apple every flice fingle, and dip
it into your batter, let your lard be very hot,
fo drop them in ; you muft keep them turning whilft enough, and mind that they be not
over brown ; as you take them out lay them
on a pewter difh before the fire whilft you
have done ; have a little white wine, butter
and fugar for the fauce ; grate over them a
little loaf fugar, and ferve them up.

163. *To make an* HERB PUDDING.

Take a good quantity of fpinage and parfley, a little forrel and mild thyme, put to
them a handful of great oatmeal creed, fhred
them together till they be very fmall, put to
them a pound of currants, well wafhed and
cleaned, four eggs well beaten in a jill of good
cream ; if you wou'd have it fweet, put in a
quarter of a pound of fugar, a little nutmeg,
a lit-

a little falt, and a handful of grated bread ;
then meal your cloth and tie it clofe before
you put it in to boil ; it will take as much
boiling as a piece of beef.

164. *To make a* PUDDING *for a* HARE.

Take the liver and chop it fmall with fome
thyme, parfley, fuer, crumbs of bread mixt
with grated nutmeg, pepper, falt, an egg,
a little fat bacon and lemon-peel; you muft
make the compofition very ftiff, left it fhould
diffolve, and you lofe your pudding.

165. *To make a* BREAD PUDDING.

Take three jills of milk, when boiled, take
a penny loaf fliced thin, cut off the out cruft,
put on the boiling milk, let it ftand clofe covered till it be cold, and beat it very well till all
the lumps be broke ; take five eggs beat
them very well, grate in a little nutmeg, fhred
fome lemon-peel, and a quarter of a pound
of butter or beef fuet, with as much fugar as
will fweeten it : and currants as many as you
pleafe ; let them be well cleaned ; fo put
them into your difh, and bake or boil it.

166. *To make* CLARE PANCAKES.

Take five or fix eggs, and beat them very
well with a little falt, put to them two or three
fpoonfuls of cream, a fpoonful of fine flour,
mix it with a little cream ; take your clare
and wafh it very clean, wipe it with a cloth,
put your eggs into a pan, juft to cover your
pan bottom, lay the clare in leaf by leaf,
whilft you have covered your pan all over ;
take a fpoon, and pour the batter over every

D 3
leaf

leaf till they are all covered; when it is done
lay the brown fide upwards, and ferve it up.

167. *To make a* LIVER PUDDING.

Take a pound of grated bread, a pound of
currants, a pound and a half of marrow and
fuet together cut fmall, three quarters of a
pound of fugar, half an ounce of cinnamon, a
quarter of an ounce of mace, a pint of grated
liver, and fome falt, mix all together ; take
twelve eggs, (leave out half of the whites)
beat them well, put to them a pint of cream,
make the eggs and cream warm, then put it
to the pudding, and ftir it well together,
fo fill them in fkins ; put to them a few
blanch'd almonds fhred fine, and a fpoonful
or two of rofe water, fo keep them for ufe.

168. *To make* OATMEAL FRITTERS.

Boil a quart of new milk, fteep a pint of
fine flour or oatmeal in it ten or twelve
hours, then beat four eggs in a little milk,
fo much as will make it like thick batter,
drop them in by fpoonfuls into frefh butter,
a fpoonful of butter in a cake, and grate
fugar over them ; have fack, butter and fugar for fauce.

169. *To make* APPLE DUMPLINGS.

Take half a dozen codlins, or any other
good apples, pare and core them, make a little
cold butter pafte, and roll it up about the
thicknefs of your finger, fo wrap round every
apple, and tie them fingle in a fine cloth,
boil them in a little falt and water, and let
the water boil before you put them in ; half
an

an hour will boil them ; you muft have for
fauce a little white wine and butter ; grate
fome fugar round the difh, and ferve them
up.

170. *To make* HERB DUMPLINGS.

Take a penny loaf, cut off the out cruft,
and the reft in flices, put to it as much hot
milk as will juft wet it, take the yolks and
whites of fix eggs, beat them with two
fpoonfuls of powder fugar, half an nutmeg,
and a little falt, fo put it to your bread ; take
half a pound of currants well cleaned, put
them to your eggs, then take a handful of the
mildeft herbs you can get, gather them fo
equal that the tafte of one be not above the
other, wafh and chop them very fmall, put as
many of them in as will make a deep green,
(don't put any parfley among them, nor any
other ftrong herb) fo mix them all together
and boil them in a cloth, make them abou
the bignefs of middling apples, about half a
hour will boil them ; put them into your difh,
and have a little candid orange, white wine,
butter and fugar for fauce, fo ferve them up.

171. *To make* MARROW TARTS.

To a quart of cream put the yolks of twelve
eggs, half a pound of fugar, fome beaten
mace and cinnamon, a little falt and fome
fack, fet it on the fire with half a pound of
bifcuits, as much marrow, a little orange-peel
and lemon-peel ; ftir it on the fire till it becomes thick, and when it is cold put it into
a difh with puff-pafte, then bake it gently
in a flow oven.   D 5   172. *To*

172. *To make* PLAIN FRUIT DUMPLINGS.

Take as much flour as you would have dumplings in quantity, put to it a spoonful of sugar, a little salt, a little nutmeg, a spoonful of light yeast, and half a pound of currants well washed and cleaned, so knead them the stiffness you do a common dumpling, you must have white wine, sugar and butter for sauce ; you may boil them either in a cloth or without ; so serve them up.

173. *To make* OYSTER LOAVES.

Take half a dozen French loaves, rasp them and make a hole at the top, take out all the crumb and fry them in butter till they be crisp ; when your oysters are stewed, put them into your loaves, cover them up before the fire to keep hot whilst you want them ; so serve them up.

They are proper either for a side-dish or middle-dish.

You may make cockle loaves or mushroom-loaves the same way.

174. *To make a* GOOSEBERRY PUDDING.

Take a quart of green gooseberries, pick, codle, bruise and rub them through a hair sieve to take out the pulp ; take six spoonfuls of the pulp, six eggs, three quarters of a pound of sugar, half a pound of clarified butter, a little lemon-peel shred fine, a handful of bread-crumbs or biscuit, a spoonful of rose-water or orange-flower-water; mix these well together, and bake it with paste round the dish ; you may add sweetmeats, if you please.

175. *To*

175. *To make an* EEL PIE.

Cafe and clean the eels, feafon them with a litle nutmeg, pepper and falt, cut them in long pieces; you muft make your pie with hot butter pafte, let it be oval with a thin cruft; lay in your eels length way, putting over them a little frefh butter; fo bake them.

Eel pies are good, and eat very well with currants, but if you put in currants you muft not ufe any black pepper, but a little Jamaica pepper.

176. *To make a* TURBOT-HEAD PIE.

Take a middling turbot-head, pretty well cut off; wafh it clean, take out the gills, feafon it pretty well with mace, pepper and falt, fo put it into a deep difh with half a pound of butter, cover it with a light puff-pafte, but lay none in the bottom; when it is baked take out the liquor and the butter that it was baked in, put it into a fauce-pan with a lump of frefh butter and flour to thicken it, with an anchovy and a glafs of white wine, fo pour it into your pie again over the fifh; you may lay round half a dozen yolks of eggs at equal diftances; when you have cut off the lid, lie it in fippets round your difb, and ferve it up.

177. *To make a Caudle for a fweet* VEAL PIE.

Take about a jill of white wine and verjuice mixed, make it very hot, beat the yolk of an egg very well, and then mix them together as you would do mull'd ale; you muft fweeten it very well, becaufe there is no fugar in the pie.   D 6   This.

This caudle will do for any other sort of pie that is sweet.

178 *To make* SWEET-MEAT TARTS.

Make a little shell-paste, roll it, and line your tins, prick them in the inside, and so bake them; when you serve 'em up put in any sort of sweet-meats, what you please.

You may have a different sort every day, do but keep your shells bak'd by you.

179. *To make* ORANGE TARTS.

Take two or three seville oranges and boil them; shift them in the boiling to take out the bitter, cut them in two, take out the pippins, and cut them in slices; they must be baked in crisp paste; when you fill the petty-pans, lay in a layer of oranges and a layer of sugar, (a pound will sweeten a dozen of small tins, if you do not put in too much orange) bake them in a slow oven, and ice them over.

180. *To make a* TANSEY *another Way*.

Take a pint of cream, some biscuits without feeds, two or three spoonfuls of fine flour, nine eggs, leaving out two of the whites, some nutmeg, and orange-flower-water, a little juice of tansey and spinage, put it into a pan till it be pretty thick, then fry or bake it, if fried take care that you do not let it be over-brown. Garnish with orange and sugar, so serve it up.

181. *A good* PASTE *for* TARTS.

Take a pint of flour, and rub a quarter of a pound of butter into it, beat two eggs with a spoonful of double-refin'd sugar, and two

two or three fpoonfuls of cream to make it
into pafte ; work it as little as you can, roll
it out thin ; butter your tins, duft on fome
flour, then lay in your pafte, and do not
fill them too full.

182. *To make* TRANSPARENT TARTS.

Take a pound of flour well dried, beat
one egg till it be very thin, then melt almoft
three quarters of a pound of butter without
falt, and let it be cold enough to mix with an
egg, then put it into the flour and make
your pafte, roll it very thin, when you are
fetting them into the oven wet them over with
a little fair water, and grate a little fugar :
if you bake them rightly they will be very fine.

183. *To make a* SHELL PASTE.

Take half a pound of fine flour, and a
quarter of a pound of butter, the yolks of
two eggs and one white, two ounces of fugar finely fifted, mix all thefe together with
a little water, and roll it very thin whilft you

d your tarts

prick them to keep them from bliftering,
make fure to roll them even, and when you
bake them ice them.

184. *To make* PASTE *for* TARTS.

Take the yolks of five or fix eggs, juft as
you would have pafte in quantity ; to the
yolks of fix eggs put a pound of butter, work
the butter with your hands whilft it take up all
the eggs, then take fome London flour
and work it with your butter whilft it comes
to a pafte, put in about two fpoonfuls of loaf
fugar

fugar beat and fifted, and about half a jill
of water ; when you have wrought it well
together it is fit for ufe.

This is a pafte that feldom runs if it be
even roll'd ; roll it thin but let your lids be
thinner than your bottoms ; when you have
made your tarts, prick them over with a pin
to keep them from bliftering ; when you are
going to put them into the oven, wet them
over with a feather dipt in fair water, and
grate over them a little double-refined loaf
fugar, it will ice them ; but don't let them
be bak'd in a hot oven.

185. *A fhort* PASTE *for* TARTS.

Take a pound of wheat-flour, and rub it
very finall three quarters of a pound of butter,
rub it as fmall as the flour, put to it three
fpoonfuls of loaf fugar beat and fifted, take
the yolks of four eggs, and beat them very
well ; put to them a fpoonful or two of rofe-
water, and as much fair water as will work
them into a pafte, then roll them thin, and
ice them over as you did the other if you
pleafe, and bake 'em in a flow oven.

186. *To make a* LIGHT PASTE *for a* VENISON
PASTY, *or other* PIE.

Take a quarter of a peck of fine flour, or
as much as you think you have occafion for,
and to every quartern of flour put a pound
and a quarter of butter, break the third part
of your butter into the flour ; then take the
whites of three or four eggs, beat them very
well to a froth, and put to them as much
water

water as will knead the meal ; do not knead it over ftiff, then roll in the reft of your butter you muft roll it five or fix times over at leaft, and ftrinkle a little fiour over your butter every time you roll it up, wrap it up the crofs way, and it will be fit for ufe.

187. *To make a Pafte for a* STANDING PIE.

Take a quartern of flour or more if you have occafion, and to every quartern of flour put a pound of butter and a little falt, knead it with boiling water, then work it very well, and let it lie whilft it is cold.

This pafte is good enough for a goofe pie, or any other ftanding-pie.

188 *A light Pafte for a* DISH PIE.

Take a quartern of flour, and break into it a pound of butter in large pieces, knead it very ftiff, handle it as lightly as you can, and roll it once or twice, then it is fit for ufe.

189. *To make* CHEESE CAKES.

Take a gallon of new milk, make of it a tender curd, wring the whey from it, put it into a bafon, and break three quarters of a pound of butter into the curd, then with a clean hand work the butter and curd together till all the butter be melted, and rub it in a hair-fieve with the back of a fpoon till all be through ; then take fix eggs, beat them with a few fpoonfuls of role-water or fack, put it into your curd with half a pound of fine fugar and a nutmeg grated ; mix them all together with a little falt, fome currants and almonds ; then work up your pafte of fine

flour

flour, with cold butter and a little fugar;
roll your pafte very thin, fill your tins with
the curd. and fet them in an oven, when they
are almoft enough take them out, then take
a quarter of a pound of butter, with a little
rofe-water, and part of a half pound of fugar, let it ftand on the coals till the butter
be melted, then pour into each cake fome of
it, fet them in the oven again till they be
brown; fo keep them for ufe.

190. *To make* GOOFER WAFERS.

Take a pound of fine flour and fix eggs,
beat them very well, put to them about a jill
of milk, mix it well with the flour, put in
half a pound of clarified butter, half a pound
of powder fugar, half of a nutmeg, and a
little falt; you may add to it two or three
fpoonfuls of cream; then take your goofer-
irons and put them into the fire to heat, when
they are hot rub them over the firft time with
a little butter in a cloth, put your batter into
one fide of your goofer-irons, put them into
the fire, and keep turning the irons every
now and then: (if your irons be too hot they
burn foon) make them a day or two before
you ufe them, only fet them down before the
fire on a pewter difh before you ferve them
up; have a little white wine and butter for
your fauce, grating fome fugar over them.

191. *To make common* CURD CHEESE CAKES.

Take a pennyworth of curds, mix them
with a little cream, beat four eggs, put to
them fix ounces of clarified butter, a quarter

of a pound of fugar, half a pound of currants
well waſh'd, and a little lemon-peel ſhred, a
little nutmeg, a ſpoonful of roſe-water or
brandy, whether you pleaſe, and a little ſalt,
mix altogether, and bake them in ſmall
petty pans.

192. CHEESE CAKES *without* CURRANTS.

Take five quarts of new milk, run it to a
tender curd, then hang it in a cloth to drain,
rub into it a pound of butter that is well
waſhed in roſe-water, put to it the yolks of
ſeven or eight eggs, and two of the whites ;
ſeaſon it with cinnamon, nutmeg and ſugar.

193. *To make a* CURD PUDDING.

Take three quarts of new milk, put to it
a little earning, as much as will break it, when
it is ſcumm'd break it down with your hand,
and when it is drained grind it with a muſtard
ball in a bowl, or beat it in a marble-mortar ;
then take half a pound of butter and ſix eggs;
leaving out three of the whites ; beat the eggs
well, and put them into the curds and butter,
grate in half a nutmeg, add a little lemon-peel
ſbred fine, and ſalt, ſweeten it to your taſte,
beat them all together, and bake them in little
petty-pans with faſt bottoms ; a quarter of an
hour will bake them ; you muſt butter the
tins very well before you put them in ; when
you diſh them up you muſt lay them the
wrong ſide upwards on the diſh, and ſtick
them with either blanch'd almonds, candid
orange or citron cut in long bits, and grate
a little loaf-ſugar over them.

194. *To make a* SLIPCOAT CHEESE.

Take five quarts of new milk, a quart of cream, and a quart of water, boil your water, then put your cream to it ; when your milk is new-milk warm put in your earning, take your curd into the ſtrainer, break it as little as you can, and let it drain, then put it into your vat, preſs it by degrees, and lay it in graſs.

195. *To make* CREAM CHEESE.

Take three quarts of new-milk, one quart of cream, and a ſpoonful of earning, put them together, let it ſtand till it come to the hardneſs of a ſtrong jelly, then put it into the mould, ſhifting it often into dry cloths, lay the weight of three pounds upon it, and about two hours after you may lay ſix or ſeven pounds upon it ; turn it often into dry cloths till night, then take the weight off, and let it lie in the mould without weight and cloth till morning, and when it is ſo dry that it doth not wet a cloth, keep it in greens till fit for uſe ; if you pleaſe you may put a little ſalt into it.

196. *To make* PIKE *eat like* STURGEON.

Take the thick part of a large pike and ſcale it, ſet on two quarts of water to boil it in, put in a jill of vinegar, a large handful of ſalt, and when it boils put in your pike, but firſt bind it about with coarſe incle ; when it is boiled you muſt not take off the incle or baiſing, but let it be on all the time it is in eating ; it muſt be kept in the ſame pickle it was boiled in, and if you think it be not ſtrong

enough

enough you muſt add a little more ſalt and vinegar, when it is cold put it upon your pike, and keep it for uſe ; before you boil the pike take out the bone.

You may do ſcate the ſame way, and in my opinion it eats more like ſturgeon.

197. *To Collar* EELS.

Take the largeſt eels you can get, ſkin and ſplit them down the belly, take out the bones, ſeaſon them with a little mace, nutmeg and ſalt ; begin at the tail and roll them up very tight, ſo bind them up in a little coarſe incle, boil it in ſalt and water, a few bay leaves, a little whole pepper, and a little alegar or vinegar; it will take an hour boiling, accord-ing as your roll is in bigneſs ; when it is boiled you muſt tie it and hang it up whilſt it be cold, then put it into the liquor that it was boiled in, and keep it for uſe.

If your eels be ſmall you may roll two or three of them together.

198. *To pot* SMELTS.

Take the freſheſt and largeſt ſmelts you can get, wipe them very well with a clean cloth, take out the guts with a ſkewer, (but you muſt not take out the milt and roan) ſeaſon them with a little mace, nutmeg and ſalt, ſo lie them in a flat pot; if you have two ſcore you muſt lay over them five ounces of butter; tie over them a paper, and ſet them in a ſlow oven ; if it be over hot it will burn them, and make them look black; an hour will bake them ; when they are baked you muſt take

them

them out and lay them on a difh to drain, and·
when they are drained you muft put them in
long pots about the length of your fmelts ;
when you lay them in you muft put betwixt
every layer the fame feafoning as you did·
before, to make them keep ; when they are
cold cover them over with clarified butter, fo
keep them for ufe.

199. *To pickle* SMELTS.

· Take the beft and largeft fmelts you can
get ; gut, wafh and wipe them, lie them in
a flat pot, cover them with a little white wine
vinegar, two or three blades of mace and a
little pepper and falt ; bake them in a flow
oven, and keep them for ufe.

200. *To ftew a* PIKE.

Take a large pike, fcale and clean it, feafon it in the belly with a little mace and falt ;
fkewer it round, put it into a deep ftew-pan,
with a pint of fmall gravy and a pint of claret, two or three blades of mace, fet it over
a ftove with a flow fire, and cover it up clofe ;·
when it is enough take part of the liquor,
put to it two anchovies, a little lemon-peel
fhred fine, and thicken the fauce with flour
and butter ; before you lie the pike on the
difh turn it with the back upwards, take off
the fkin, and ferve it up. Garnifh your difh
with lemon and pickle.

201. SAUCE *for a* PIKE.

Take a little of the liquor that comes from
the pike when you take it out of the oven,
put to it two or three anchovies, a little lemon-peel

mon-peel fhred, a fpoonful or two of white wine, or a little juice of lemon, which you pleafe, put to it fome butter and flour, make your fauce about the thicknefs of cream, put it into a bafon or filver-boat, and fet it in your difh with your pike, you may lay round your pike any fort of fried fifh, or broiled, if you have it; you may have the fame fauce for a broiled pike, only add a little good gravy, a few fhred capers, a little parfley, and a fpoonful or two of oyfter and cockle pickle if you have it.

202. *How to roaft a* PIKE *with a Pudding in the Belly.*

Take a large pike, fcale and clean it, draw it at the gills.——*To make a pudding for the pike.* Take a large handful of bread-crumbs, as much beef-fuet fhred fine, two eggs, a little pepper and falt, a little grated nutmeg, a little parfley, fweet-marjoram and lemon-peel fhred fine; fo mix altogether, put it into the belly of your pike, fkewer it round and lie it in an earthen difh with a lump of butter over it, a little falt and flour, fo fet it in the oven; an hour will roaft it.

203. *To drefs a* COD'S HEAD.

Take a cod's head, wafh and clean it, take out the gills, cut it open, and make it to lie flat; (if you have no conveniency of boiling it you may do it in an oven, and it will be as well or better) put it into a copper-difh or earthen one, lie upon it a little butter, falt, and

and flour, and when it is enough take off
the ſkin.

SAUCE *for the* COD'S HEAD.

Take a little white gravy, about a pint of
oyſters or cockles, a little ſhred lemon-peel,
two or three ſpoonfuls of white wine, and a-
bout half a pound of butter thicken'd with
flour, and put it into your boat or baſon.

Another SAUCE *for a* COD'S HEAD.

Take a pint of good gravy, a lobſter or
crab, which you can get, dreſs and put it into
your gravy with a little butter, juice of lemon, ſhred lemon-peel, and a few ſhrimps
if you have them; thicken it with a little
flour, and put it into your baſon, ſet the
oyſters on one ſide of the diſh and this on the
other; lay round the head boiled whitings,
or any fried fiſh; pour over the head a little melted butter. Garniſh your diſh with
horſe-radiſh, ſlices of lemon and pickles.

204. *To ſtew* CARP *or* TENCH.

Take your carp or tench and waſh them,
ſcale the carp but not the tench, when you
have cleaned them wipe them with a cloth,
and fry them in a frying pan with a little butter to harden the ſkin; before you put them
into the ſtew-pan, put to them a little good
gravy, the quantity will be according to the
largeneſs of your fiſh, with a jill of claret,
three or four anchovies at leaſt, a little ſhred
lemon-peel, a blade or two of mace, let all
ſtew together, till your carp be enough, over
a ſlow fire; when it is enough take part of
the

the liquor, put to it half a pound of butter, and thicken it with a little flour; so serve it up. Garnish your dish with crisp parsley, slices of lemon and pickles.

If you have not the convenience of stewing them, you may broil them before a fire; only make the same sauce.

205. *How to make* SAUCE *for a boiled* SALMON *or* TURBOT.

Take a little mild white gravy, two or three anchovies, a spoonful of oyster or cockle pickle, a little shred lemon peel, half a pound of butter, a little parsley and fennel shred small, and a little juice of lemon, but not too much, for fear it should take off the sweetness.

206. *To make* SAUCE *for* HADDOCK *or* COD, *either broiled or boiled.*

Take a little gravy, a few cockles, oysters or mushrooms, put to them a little of the gravy that comes from the fish, either broiled or boiled, it will do very well if you have no other gravy, a little catchup and a lump of butter; if you have neither oysters nor cockles you may put in an anchovy or two, and thicken with flour; you may put in a few shred capers, or a little mango, if you have it.

207. *To stew* EELS.

Take your eels, case, clean and skewer them round, put them into a stew-pan with a little good gravy, a little claret to redden the gravy, a blade or two of mace, an anchovy,

and

and a little lemon-peel; when they are enough thicken them with a little flour and butter. Garnifh your difh with parfley.

208. *To fpitch-cock* EELS.

Take your eels, cafe and clean them, feafon them with nutmeg, pepper and falt, fkewer them round, broil them before the fire, and bafte them with a little butter; when they are almoft enough ftrinkle them over with a little fhred parfley, and make your fauce of a little gravy, butter, anchovy, and a little oyfter pickle if you have it ; don't pour the fauce over your eels, put it into a china bafon, and fet it in the middle of your difh.

Garnifh with crifp parfley, and ferve them up.

209. *To boil* HERRINGS.

Take your herrings, fcale and wafh them, take out the milt and roan, fkewer them round, and tie them with a ftring or elfe they will come loofe in the boiling and be fpoil'd; fet on a pretty broad ftew-pan, with as much water as will cover them, put to it a little falt, lie in your herrings with the backs downwards, boil with them the milt and roans to lie round them ; they will boil in half a quarter of an hour over a flow fire ; when they are boiled take them up with an egg flice, fo turn them over and fet them to drain. Make your fauce of a little gravy and butter, an anchovy, and a little boiled parfley fbred; put it into the bafon, fet it in the middle of the difh, lie the herrings round with their tails towards the

bafon, and lie the milts and roans between
every herring. Garnifh with crifp parfley
and lemon ; fo ferve them up.

210. To fry HERRINGS.

Scale and wafh your herrings clean, ftrew
over them a little flour and falt; let your
butter be very hot before you put your herrings into the pan, then fhake them to keep
them ftirring, and fry them over a brifk fire ;
when they are fried cut off the heads and bruife
them, put to them a jill of ale, (but the ale
muft not be bitter) add a little pepper and
falt, a fmall onion or fhalot, if you have
them, and boil them altogether ; when they
are boiled, ftrain them, and put them into
your fauce-pan again, thicken them with a
little flour and butter, put it into a bafon,
and fet it in the middle of your difh ; fry
the milts and roans together, and lay round
your herrings. Garnifh your difh with crifp
parfley, and ferve it up.

211. To pickle HERRINGS.

Scale and clean your herrings, take out the
milts and roans, and fkewer them round,
feafon them with a little pepper and falt, put
them in a deep pot, cover them with alegar,
put to them a little whole Jamaica pepper,
and two or three bay leaves ; bake them and
keep them for ufe.

212. To ftew OYSTERS.

Take a feote or two of oyfters, according
as you have occafion, put them into a fmall
ftew-pan, with a few bread-crumbs, a little
water,

up.

213. *To fry* OYSTERS.

Take a fcore or two of the largeft oyfters you can get, and the yolks of four or five eggs, beat them very well, put to them a little nutmeg, pepper and falt, a fpoonful of fine flour, and a little raw parfley fhred, fo dip in your oyfters, and fry them in butter a light brown.

They are very proper to lie about either ftew'd oyfters, or any other fifh, or made difhes.

214. OYSTERS *in* SCALLOP SHELLS.

Take half a dozen fmall fcallop fhells, lay in the bottom of every fhell a lump of butter, a few bread-crumbs, and then your oyfters; laying over them again a few more bread-crumbs, a little butter, and a little beat pepper, fo fet them to crifp, either in the oven or before the fire, and ferve them up.

They are proper for either a fide-difh or middle-difh.

215. *To keep* HERRINGS *all the Year.*

Take frefh herrings, cut off their heads, open and wafh them very clean, feafon them with falt, black pepper, and Jamaica pepper, put them into a pot, cover them with white wine vinegar and water, of each an equal

quantity,

quantity, and fet them in a flow oven to
bake; tie the pot up clofe and they will keep
a year in the pickle.

216. *To make artificial* Sturgeon *another Way.*

Take out the bones of a turbot or bret,
lay it in falt twenty four hours, boil it with
good ftore of falt; make your pickle of white
wine vinegar and three quarts of water,
boil them, and put in a little vinegar in the
boiling; don't boil it over much, if you do
it will make it foft ; when 'tis enough take
it out till it be cold, put the fame pickle to
it, and keep it for ufe.

217. *To ftew* MUSHROOMS.

Take mufhrooms, and clean them, the buttons you may wafh, but the flaps you muft
peel both infide and out; when you have cleaned them, pick out the little ones for pickling, and cut the reft in pieces for ftewing;
wafh them and put them into a little water ;
give them a boil and it will take off the faint-
nefs, fo drain from them all the water, then
put them into a pan with a lump of butter,
a little fhred mace, pepper and falt to your
tafte (putting to them a little water) hang
them over a flow fire for half an hour, when
they are enough thicken them with a little
flour ; ferve them up with fippets.

218. *To make* ALMOND PUFFS.

Take a pound of almonds blanch'd, and
beat them with orange-flower water, then
take a pound of fugar, and boil them almoft
to a candy height, put in your almonds and

E   ftir

ftir them on the fire, keep ftirring them till
they be ftiff, then take them off the fire and
ftir them till they be cold; beat them a quarter
of an hour in a mortar, putting to them a
pound of fugar lifted, and a little lemon-peel
grated, make it into a pafte with the whites
of three eggs, and beat it into a froth more
or lefs as you think proper; bake them in an
oven almoft cold, and keep them for ufe.

219. *To pot* MUSHROOMS.

Take the largeft mufhrooms, fcrape and
clean them, put them into your pan with a
lump of butter, and a little falt, let them
ftew over a flow fire whilft they are enough,
put to them a little mace and whole pepper,
then dry them with a cloth, and put them
down into a pot as clofe as you can, and as
you lie them down ftrinkle in a little falt and
mace, when they are cold cover them over
with butter; when you ufe them tofs them
up with gravy, a few bread crumbs and butter; do not make your pot over large, but
rather put them into two pots; they will
keep the better if you take the gravy from
them when they are ftewed.

They are good for fifh-fauce, or any other
whilft they are frefh.

220. *To fry* TROUT; *or any other Sort of Fifh.*

Take two or three eggs, more or lefs according as you have fifh to fry, take the fifh
and cut it in thin flices, lie it upon a board,
rub the eggs over it with a feather, and ftrew
on a little flour and falt, fry it in fine drip-

pings

pings or butter, let the drippings be very hot before you put in the fish, but do not let it burn, if you do it will make the fish black; when the fish is in the pan, you may do the other fide with the egg, and as you fry it lay it to drain before the fire till all be fried, then it is ready for ufe.

221. *To make* SAUCE *for* SALMON *or* TURBOT.

Boil your turbot or falmon, and fet it to drain; take the gravy that drains from the falmon or turbot, an anchovy or two, a little lemon-peel fhred, a fpoonful of catchup, and a little butter, thicken it with flour the thicknefs of cream, put to it a little fhred parfley and fennel; but do not put in your parfley and fennel till you be juft going to fend it up, for it will take off the green.

The gravy of all forts of fifh is a great addition to your fauce, if the fifh be fweet.

222. *To drefs* COD'S ZOONS.

Lie them in water all night, and then boil them, if they be falt fhift them once in the boiling, when they are tender cut them in long pieces, drefs them up with eggs as you do falt fifh, take one or two of them and cut into fquare pieces, dip them in egg and fry them to lay round your difh.

It is proper to lie about any other difh.

223. *To make* SOLOMON GUNDY *to eat in Lent*.

Take five or fix white herrings, lay them in water all night, boil them as foft as you would do for eating, and fhift them in the boiling to take out the faltnefs; when they are

E 2   boiled

boiled take the fiſh from the bone, and mind
you don't break the bones in pieces, leaving
on the head and tail; take the white part of
the herrings, a quarter of a pound of anchovies, a large apple, a little onion ſhred
fine, or ſhalot, and a little lemon-peel,
ſhred them all together, and lie them over the
bones on both ſides, in the ſhape of a herring; then take off the peel of a lemon very
thin, and cut it in long bits, juſt as it will
reach over the herrings; you muſt lie this
peel over every herring pretty thick. Garniſh your diſb with a few pickled oyſters,
capers, and muſhrooms, if you have any; ſo
ſerve them up.

224. SOLOMON GUNDY *another Way*.

Take the white part of a turkey, or other
fowl; if you have neither, take a little white
veal and mince it pretty ſmall; take a little
hang beef or tongues, ſcrape them very fine,
a few ſhred capers, and the yolks of four or
five eggs ſhred ſmall; take a delf diſh and
lie a delf plate in the diſh with the wrong
ſide up, ſo lie on your meat and other ingredients, all ſingle in quarters, one to anſwer
another; ſet in the middle a large lemon or
mango, ſo lie round your diſh anchovies in
lumps, pickled oyſters or cockles, and a
few pickled muſhrooms, ſlices of lemon and
capers; ſo ſerve it up.

This is proper for a ſide-diſh either at
noon or night.

225. *To*

225. *To make* LEMON CHEESE CAKES.

Blanch half a pound of almonds, and beat them in a ftone mortar very fine, with a little rofe-water ; put in eight eggs, leaving out five of the whites ; take three quarters of a pound of fugar, and three quarters of a pound of butter melted, beat all together, then take three lemon fkins, boiled tender, the rind and all, beat them very well, and mix them with the reft, then put them into your pafte.

You may make a lemon-pudding the fame way, only add the juice of half a lemon : Before you fet them in the oven, grate over them a little fine loaf fugar.

226. *To make white* GINGER BREAD.

Take a little gum-dragon, lay it in rofe-water all night, then take a pound of jordan almonds blanch'd with a little of the gum-water, a pound of double-refined fugar beat and fifted, an ounce of cinnamon beat with a little rofe-water, work it into a pafte and print it, then fet it in a ftove to dry.

227. *To make red* GINGER BREAD.

Take a quart and a jill of red wine, a jill and a half of brandy, feven or eight manfhets, according to the fize the bread is, grate them, (the cruft muft be dried, beat and fifted) three pounds and a half of fugar beat and fifted, two ounces of cinnamon, and two ounces of ginger beat and fifted, a pound of almonds blanched and beat with rofe-water, put the bread into the liquor by degrees, ftirring it

E 3 all

all the time, when the bread is all well mix'd take it off the fire ; you muſt put the ſugar, ſpices, and almonds into it, when it is cold print it ; keep ſome of the ſpice to duſt the prints with.

228. *To make a* GREAT CAKE.

Take five pounds of fine flour, (let it be dried very well before the fire) and ſix pounds of currants well dreſs'd and rub'd in cloths after they are waſh'd, ſet them in a ſieve before the fire ; you muſt weigh your currants after they are cleaned, then take three quarters of an ounce of mace, two large nutmegs beaten and mix'd amongſt the flour, a pound of powder ſugar, a pound of citron, and a pound of candid orange, (cut your citron and orange in pretty large pieces) and a pound of almonds cut in three or four pieces long way ; then take ſixteen eggs, leaving out half of the whites, beat your ſugar and eggs for half an hour with a little ſalt ; take three jills of cream, and three pounds and a half of butter, melt your butter with part of the cream for fear it ſhould be too hot, put in between a jack and a jill of good brandy, a quart of light yeaſt, and the reſt of the cream, mix all your liquors together about blood-warm, make a hole in the middle of your flour, and put in the liquids, cover it half an hour and let it ſtand to riſe, then put in your currants and mix all together ; butter your hoop, tie a paper three fold, and put it at the bottom in your hoop ; juſt when they are ready to ſet

in

in the oven, put the cake into your hoop at three times; when you have laid a little pafte at the bottom, lay in part of your fweet-meats and almonds, then put in a little pafte over them again, and the reft of your fweet-meats and almonds; then lay on the reft of your pafte, and fet it in a quick oven; two hours will bake it.

229. *To make* ICEING *for this* CAKE.

Take two pounds of double-refined fugar, beat it, and fift it through a fine fieve; put to it a fpoonful of fine ftarch, a pennyworth of gum-arabic, beat them all well together; take the whites of four or five eggs, beat them well, and put to them a fpoonful of rofe-water, or orange-flower water, a fpoon-ful of the juice of lemon, beat them with the whites of your eggs, and put in a little to your fugar till you wet it, then beat them for two hours whilft your cake is baking; if you make it over thin it will run; when you lie it on your cake you muft lie it on with a knife; if you would have the iceing very thick, you muft add a little more fugar; wipe off the loofe currants before you put on the ieeing, and put it into the oven to harden the iceing.

230. *To make a* PLUMB CAKE.

Take five pounds of flour, dried and cold, mix to it an ounce of mace, half an ounce of cinnamon, a quarter of an ounce of nut-megs, half a quarter of an ounce of lemon-peel grated, and a pound of fine fugar; take fifteen eggs, leaving out feven of the whites,

E 4 beat

beat your eggs with half a jill of brandy or
fack, a little orange-flower water, or rofe
water; then put to your eggs near a quart
of light yeaft, fet it on the fire with a quart
of cream, and three pounds of butter, let
your butter melt in the cream, fo let it ftand
till new milk warm, then fkim off all the butter
and moft of the milk, and mix it to your eggs
and yeaft; make a hole in the middle of
your flour, and put in your yeaft, ftrinkle
at the top a little flour, then mix to it a
little falt, fix pounds of currants well wafh'd,
clean'd, dry'd, pick'd, and plump'd by the
fire, a pound of the beft raifins ftoned, and
beat them altogether whilft they leave the
bowl; put in a pound of candid orange, and
half a pound of citron cut in long pieces;
then butter the girth and fill it full; bake it
in a quick oven, againft it be enough have
an iceing ready.

231. *To make a* Caraway Cake.

Take eighteen eggs, leave out half of the
whites, and beat them; take two pounds of
butter, wafh the butter clear from milk and
falt, put to it a little rofe-water, and work
your butter very well with your hands till it
take up all the eggs, then mix them in half a
jack of brandy and fack; grate into your
eggs a lemon rind; put in by degrees (a
fpoonful at a time) two pounds of fine flour,
a pound and a half of loaf-fugar, that is
fifted and dry; when you have mixed them
very well with your hands, take a thible and

beat

beat it very well for half an hour, till it look very white, then mix to it a few feeds, fix ounces of caraway comfits, and half a pound of citron and candid orange ; then beat it well, butter your girth, and put it in a quick oven.

232. *To make* CAKES *to keep all the Year.*

Have in readinefs a pound and four ounces of flour well dried, take a pound of butter unfalted, work it with a pound of white fugar till it cream, three fpoonfuls of fack, and the rind of an orange, boil it till it is not bitter, and beat it with fugar, work thefe together, then clean your hands, and grate a nutmeg into your flour, put in three eggs and two whites, mix them well, then with a pafte-pin or thible ftir in your flour to the butter, make them up into little cakes, wet the top with fack and ftrew on fine fugar ; bake them on buttered papers, well floured, but not too much ; you may add a pound of currants wafhed and warmed.

233. *To make* SHREWSBERRY CAKES.

Take two pounds of fine flour, put to it a pound and a quarter of butter (rub them very well) a pound and a quarter of fine fugar fifted, grate in a nutmeg, beat in three whites of eggs and two yolks, with a little rofe-water, and fo knead your pafte with it, let it lay an hour, then make it up into cakes, prick them and lay them on papers, wet them with a feather dip'd in rofe-water, and grate over

E 5

them

them a little fine fugar ; bake them in a flow
oven, either on tins or paper.

234. *To make a fine* CAKE.

Take five pounds of fine flour dried, and
keep it warm ; four pounds of loaf-fugar
pounded, fifted and warmed; five pounds of
currants well cleaned and warmed before the
fire ; a pound and a half of almonds blanch'd,
beat, dried, flit and kept warm; five pounds
of good butter well wafh'd and beat from the
water ; then work it an hour and a half till
it comes to a fine cream ; put to the butter
all the fugar, work it up, and then the flour,
put in a pint of brandy, then all the whites
and yolks of the eggs, mix all the currants
and almonds with the reft. There muft
be four pounds of eggs in weight in the
fhells, the yolks and the whites beat them
feparate, the whites beat to a froth ; you
muft not ceafe beating till they are beat to a
curd, to prevent oiling; to this quantity of
cake put a pound and a half of orange-peel
and citron fhred, without plumbs, and half
a pound of caraway feeds, it will require
four hours baking, and the oven muft be
as hot as for bread, but let it be well flaked
when it has remained an hour in the oven,
and ftop it clofe ; you may ice it if you pleafe.

235. *To make a* SEED CAKE.

Take one quartern of fine flour well dried before the fire, when it is cold rub in a
pound of butter ; take three quarters of a
pound of caraway comfits, fix fpoonfuls of

new.

new yeaft, fix fpoonfuls of cream, the yolks of fix eggs and two whites, and a little fack ; mix all thefe together in a very light pafte, fet it before the fire till it rife, and fo bake it in a tin.

236. *To make an ordinary* PLUMB CAKE.

Take a pound of flour well dried before the fire, a pound of currants, two penny-worth of mace and cloves, two eggs, four fpoonfuls of good new yeaft, half a pound of butter, half a pint of cream, melt the butter, warm the cream, and mix altogether in a very light pafte, butter your tin before you put it in ; an hour will bake it.

237. *To make an* ANGELICA CAKE.

Take the ftalks of angelica boil and green them very well, put to every pound of pulp a pound of loaf-fugar beaten very well, and when you think it is beaten enough, lay them in what fafhion you pleafe on glaffes, and as they candy turn them.

238. *To make* KING CAKES.

Take a pound of flour, three quarters of a pound of butter, half a pound of fugar and half a pound of currants, well cleaned ; rub your butter well into your flour, and put in as many yolks of eggs as will lithe them, then put in your fugar, currants, and fome mace, fhred in as much as will give them a tafte, fo make them up in little round cakes, and butter the papers you lie them on.

239. *To make* BREAKFAST CAKES.

Take a pound of currants well wafhed,

E 6

(rub

(rub them in a cloth till dry) a pound of flour dried before a fire, take three eggs, leave out one of the whites, four spoonfuls of new yeaft, and four spoonfuls of fack or two of brandy, beat the yeaft and eggs well together ; then take a jill of cream, and fomething above a quarter of a pound of butter, fet them on a fire, and ftir them till the butter be melted, (but do not let them boil) grate a large nutmeg into the flour, with currants, and five spoonfuls of fugar ; mix all together, beat it with your hand till it leave the bowl, then flour the tins you put the pafte in, and let them ftand a little to rife, then bake them an hour and a quarter.

240. To make MACAROONS.

Take a pound of blanched almonds and beat them, put fome rofe-water in while beating; (they muft not be beaten too fmall) mix them with the whites of five eggs, a pound of fugar finely beaten and fifted, and a handful of flour, mix all thefe very well together, lay them on wafers, and bake them in a very temperate oven, (it muft not be fo hot as for manchet) then they are fit for ufe.

241. To make WIGGS.

Take two pounds of flour, a pound of butter, a pint of cream, four eggs, (leaving out two of the whites) and two fpoonfuls of yeaft, fet them to rife a little; when they are mixed add half a pound of fugar, and half a pound of caraway comfits, make them up with

with fugar and bake them in a dripping
pan..

242. To make Raspberry Cream.

Take rafpberries, bruife them, put 'em in a
pan on a quick fire whilft the juice be dried
up, then take the fame weight of fugar as
you have of rafpberries, and fet them on a flow
fire, let them boil whilft they are pretty ftiff;
make them into cakes, and dry them near
the fire, or in the fun.

243. To make Queen Cakes.

Take a pound of London flour dry'd well
before the fire, nine eggs, a pound of loaf
fugar, beaten and lifted, put one half to your
eggs and the other to your butter; take a
pound of butter and melt it without water, put
it into a ftone bowl, when it is almoft cold put
in your fugar, and a fpoonful or two of rofe
water, beat it very quick for half an hour,
till it be as white as cream; beat the eggs
and fugar as long and very quick, whilft they
be white; when they are well beat mix them
all together; then take half a pound of currants
cleaned well, and a little fhred mace, fo you
may fill one part of your tins before you put
in your currants; you may put a quarter of
a pound of almonds fhred (if you pleafe)
into them that is without the currants; you
may ice them if you pleafe, but do not let
the iceing be thicker than you may lie on
with a little brufh.

244. To make a Biscuit Cake.

Take a pound of London flour dry'd before

fore the fire, a pound of loaf fugar beaten
and fifted, beat nine eggs and a fpoonful or
two of rofe water with the fugar for two
hours, then put them to your flour and mix
them well together ; put in an ounce of caraway feeds, then put it into your tin and
bake it an hour and a half in a pretty quick
oven.

245. *To make* CRACKNELS.

Take half a pound of fine flour, half a
pound of fugar, two ounces of butter, two
eggs, and a few caraway feeds ; (you muft
beat and fift the fugar) then put it to your
flour and work it to pafte ; roll them as thin
as you can, and cut them out with queen
cake tins, lie them on papers and bake them
in a flow oven.

They are proper to eat with chocolate.

246. *To make* PORTUGAL CAKES.

Take a pound of flour, a pound of butter, a pound of fugar, a pound of currants
well cleaned, and a nutmeg grated ; take half
of the flour and mix it with fugar and nutmeg, melt the butter and put into it the yolks
of eight eggs very well beat, and only four
of the whites, and as the froth rifes put it
into the flour, and do fo till all is in ; then
beat it together, ftill ftrewing in fome of
the other half of the flour, and beat it till
all the flour be in, then butter the pans and
fill them, but do not bake them too much ;
you may ice them if you pleafe, or you may
ftrew caraway comfits of all forts on them
when

when they go into the oven. The currants
muſt be plump'd in warm water, and dried
before the fire, then put them into your
cakes.

247. *To make* PLUMB-CAKES *another Way.*

Take two pounds of butter, beat it with a
little roſe water and orange-flour-water till
it be like cream, two pounds of flour dried
before the fire, a quarter of an ounce of
mace, a nutmeg, half a pound of loaf ſugar, beat and ſifted, fifteen eggs (beat the
whites by themſelves and yolks with your
ſugar) a jack of brandy and as much ſack,
two pounds of currants very well cleaned, and
half a pound of almonds blanch'd and cut in
two or three pieces length way, ſo mix all
together, and put it into your hoop or tin;
you may put in half a pound of candid orange
and citron if you pleaſe; about an hour will
bake it in a quick oven; if you have a mind
to have it iced a pound of ſugar will ice it.

248. *To make a* GINGER BREAD CAKE.

Take two pounds of treacle, two pounds
and a quarter of flour, an ounce of beat
ginger, three quarters of a pound of ſugar,
two ounces of coriander ſeeds, two eggs, a
pennyworth of new ale with the yeaſt on it,
a glaſs of brandy, and two ounces of lemon-
peel, mix all theſe together in a bowl, and ſet
it to riſe for half an hour, then put it into a
tin to bake, and wet it with a little treacle
and water; if you have a quick oven an
hour and a half will bake it.

249. *To*

249. *To make* CHOCOLATE CREAM.

Take four ounces of chocolate, more or lefs, according as you would have your difh in bignefs, grate it and boil it in a pint of cream, then mill it very well with a chocolate ftick ; take the yolks of two eggs and beat them very well, leaving out the ftrain, put to them three or four fpoonfuls of cream, mix them all together, fet it on the fire, and keep ftirring it till it thicken, but do not let it boil ; you muft fweeten it to your tafte, and keep ftirring it till it be cold, fo put it into your glaffes or china difhes, which you pleafe.

250. *To make white* LEMON CREAM.

Take a jill of fpring water and a pound of fine fugar, fet it over a fire till the fugar and water be diffolv'd, then put the juice of four good lemons to your fugar and water, the whites of four eggs well beat, fet it on the fire again, and keep it ftirring one way till it juft fimmers and does not boil, ftrain it thro' a fine cloth, then put it on the fire again, adding to it a fpoonful of orange-flower water, ftir it till it thickens on a flow fire, then ftrain into bafons or glaffes for your ufe; do not let it boil, if you do it will curdle.

251. *To make* CREAM CURDS.

Take a gallon of water, put to it a quart of new milk, and a little falt, a pint of fweet cream and eight eggs, leaving out half of the whites and ftrains, beat them very well, put to them a pint of four cream, mix them very

well

well together, and when your pan is juft at boiling (but it muft not boil) put in the four cream and your eggs, ftir it about to keep it from fettling to the bottom; let it ftand whilft it begins to rife up, then have a little fair water, and as they rife keep putting it in whilft they be well rifen, then take them off the fire, and let them ftand a little to fadden; have ready a fieve with a clean cloth over it, and take up the curds with a ladle or egg-flicer, whether you have; you muft always make them the night before you ufe them; this quantity will make a large difh if your cream be good; if you think your curds be too thick, mix to them two or three fpoonfuls of good cream, lie them upon a china difh in lumps; fo ferve them up.

252. To make APPLE CREAM.

Take half a dozen large apples, (codlings or any other apples that will be foft) and coddle them; when they are cold take out the pulp; then take the whites of four or five eggs, (leaving out the ftrains) three quarters of a pound of double-refined fugar beat and fifted, a fpoonful or two of rofe-water and grate in a little lemon-peel, fo beat all together for an hour, whilft it be white, then lay it on a china difh, fo ferve it up.

253. To fry CREAM to eat hot.

Take a pint of cream and boil it, three fpoonfuls of London flour, mix'd with a little milk, put in three eggs, and beat them very well with the flour, a little falt, a

fpoon-

spoonful or two of fine powder sugar, mix
them very well; then put your cream to them
on the fire and boil it; then beat two eggs
more very well, and when you take your pan
off the fire stir them in, and pour them into
a large pewter dish, about half an inch thick;
when it is quite cold cut it out in square bits,
and fry it in butter, a light brown; as you fry
them set them before the fire to keep hot and
crisp, so dish them up with a little white
wine, butter and sugar for your sauce, in a
china cup, set it in the midst, and grate over
some loaf sugar.

254. *To make* RICE *or* ALMOND CREAM.

Take two quarts of cream, boil it with
what seasoning you please, then take it from
the fire and sweeten it, pick out the seasoning and divide it into two parts, take a quarter of a pound of blanch'd almonds well beat
with orange flower water, set that on the
fire, and put to it the yolks of four eggs
well beat and strained, keep it stirring all the
time it is on the fire, when it rises to boil
take it off, stir it a little, then put it into your
bason, the other half set on the fire, and
thicken it with flour of rice; when you
take it off put to it the juice of a lemon,
orange-flower water or sack, and stir it till
it be cold, then serve it up.

255. *To make* CALF'S FOOT JELLY.

Take four calf's feet and dress them, boil
them in six quarts of water over a slow fire,
whilst all the bones will come out, and half
the

the water be boiled away, ſtrain it into a
ſtone-bowl, then put to them two or three
quarts more water, and let it boil away to
one : If you want a large quantity of flummery or jelly at one time, take two calf's
feet more, it will make your ſtoek the ſtrong-
er; you muſt make your ſtock the day before
you uſe it, and before you put your ſtoek into
the pan take off the fat, and put it into
your pan to melt, take the whites of eight or
ten eggs, juſt as you have jelly in quantity,
(for the more whites you have makes your
jelly the finer) .beat your whites to a froth,
and put to them five or fix lemons, according
as they are of goodneſs, a little white wine
or rheniſh, mix them well together (but let
not your ſtock be too hot when you put them
in) and ſweeten it to your taſte ; keep it ſtir-
ing all the time whilſt it boil; take your bag
and dip it in hot water, and wring it well
out, then put in your jelly, and keep it ſhifting whilſt it comes clear ; throw a lemon-
peel or two into your bag as the jelly is com-
ing off, and put in ſome bits of peel into your
glaſſes.

You may make hartſhorn jelly the ſame
way.

256. To make ORANGE CREAM.

Take two ſevile oranges, and peel them
very thin, put the peel into a pint of fair
water, and let it lie for an hour or two ; take
four eggs, and beat them very well, put to
them the juice of three or four oranges, according

according as they are in goodneſs, and ſweeten
them with double refin'd ſugar to your taſte,
mix the water and ſugar together, and ſtrain
them thro' a fine cloth into your tankard,
and ſet it over the fire as you did the lemon
cream, and put it into your glaſſes for uſe.

257. *To make yellow* Lemon Cream,

Take two or three lemons, according as
they are in bigneſs, take off the peel as thin
as you can from the white, put it into a pint
of clear water, and let it lie three or four
hours; take the yolks of three or four eggs,
beat them very well, about eight ounces of
double refin'd ſugar, put it into your water
to diſſolve, and a ſpoonful or two of roſe-
water or orange-flower-water, which you can
get, mix all together with the juice of two of
your lemons, and if your lemons prove not
good, put in the juice of three, ſo ſtrain them
through a fine cloth into a ſilver tankard,
and ſet it over a ſtove or chafing diſb, ſtirring it all the time, and when it begins to be
as thick as cream take it off, but don't let it
boil, if you do it will curdle, ſtir it whilſt it
be cold, and put it into glaſſes for uſe.

258. *To make white* Lemon Cream *another
way.*

Take a pint of ſpring water, and the
whites of fix eggs, beat them very well to a
froth, put them to your water, adding to it
half a pound of double refin'd ſugar, a ſpoonful of orange-flower water, and the juice of
three lemons, ſo mix all together, and ſtrain
them

them through a fine cloth into your filver tankard, fet it over a flow fire in a chafing difh, and keep ftirring it all the time ; as you fee it thickens take it off, it will fooner curdle than be yellow, ftir it whilft it be cold, and put it in fmall jelly glaffes for ufe.

259. To make SAGO CUSTARDS.

Take two ounces of fago, wafh it in a little water, fet it on to cree in a pint of milk, and let it cree till it be tender, when it is cold put to it three jills of cream, boil it altogether with a blade or two of mace, or a ftick of cinnamon ; take fix eggs, leave out the ftrains, beat them very well, mix a little of your cream amongft your eggs, then mix altogether, keep ftirring it as you put it in, fo fet it over a flow fire, and ftir it about whilft it be the thicknefs of a good cream ; you muft not let it boil ; when you take it off the fire put in a tea cup full of brandy, and fweeten it to your tafte, then put it into pots or glaffes for ufe. You may have half the quantity if you pleafe.

260. To make ALMOND CUSTARDS.

Boil two quarts of fweet cream with a ftick of cinnamon ; take eight eggs, leaving out all the whites but two, beat them very well ; take fix ounces of Jordan almonds, blanch and beat them with a little rofe-water, fo give them a boil in your cream; put in half a pound of powder fugar, and a little of your cream amongft your eggs, mix altogether, and fet them over a flow fire, ftir it all the time whilft it be as thick as cream, but don't

let

let it boil ; when you take it off put in a little
brandy to your tafte, fo put it into your cups
for ufe,

You may make rice-cuftard the fame way.

261. *To make a* SACK POSSET.

Take a quart of cream, boil it with two
or three blades of mace, and grate in a long
bifcuit ; take eight eggs, leave out half the
whites, beat them very well, and a pint of
goofeberry wine, make it hot, fo mix it well
with your eggs, fet it over a flow fire, and
ftir it about whilft it be as thick as cuftard ; fet
a difh that is deep over a ftove, put in your
fack and eggs, when your cream is boiling
hot, put it to your fack by degrees, and ftir
it all the time it ftands over your ftove,
whilft it be thoroughly hot, but don't let it
boil ; you muft make it about half an hour
before you want it ; fet it upon a hot hearth,
and then it will be as thick as cuftard ; make
a little froth of cream, to lay over the poffet ; when you difh it up fweeten it to your
tafte ; you may make it without bifcuit if
you pleafe, and don't lay on your froth till
you ferve it up.

262. *To make a* LEMON POSSET.

Take a pint of good thick cream, grate
into it the outermoft fkin of two lemons, and
fqueeze the juice into a jack of white wine,
and fweeten it to your tafte ; take the whites
of two eggs without the ftrains, beat them to
a froth, fo whifk them altogether in a ftone
bowl for half an hour, then put them into
glaffes for ufe. 263. *To*

263. *To make whipt* SILLABUBS.

Take two porringers of cream and one of white wine, grate in the skin of a lemon, take the whites of three eggs, sweeten it to your taste, then whip it with a whisk, take off the froth as it rises, and put it into your sillabub-glasses or pots, whether you have, then they are fit for use.

264. *To make* ALMOND BUTTER.

Take a quart of cream, and half a pound of almonds, beat them with the cream, then strain it, and boil it with twelve yolks of eggs and two whites, till it curdle, hang it up in a cloth till morning and then sweeten it; you may rub it through a sieve with the back of a spoon, or strain it through a coarse cloth.

265. *To make* BLACK CAPS.

Take a dozen of middling pippins and cut them in two, take out the cores and black ends, lay them with the flat side downwards, set them in the oven, and when they are about half roasted take them out, wet them over with a little rose water, and grate over them loaf sugar, pretty thick, set them into the oven again, and let them stand till they are black; when you serve them up, put them either into cream or custard, with the black side upwards, and set them at equal distances.

266. *To make* SAUCE *for tame* DUCKS.

Take the necks and gizzards of your ducks, a scrag of mutton if you have it, and make a little sweet gravy, put to it a few
bread-

bread crumbs, a small onion, and a little whole pepper, boil them for half a quarter of an hour, put to them a lump of butter, and if it is not thick enough a little flour, so salt it to your taste.

267. *To make* Sauce *for a* Green Goose.

Take a little good gravy, a little butter, and a few scalded gooseberries, mix all toge-ther, and put it on the dish with your goose.

268. *To make another* Sauce *for a* Green-Goose.

Take the juice of sorrel, a little butter, and a few scalded gooseberries, mix them to-gether, and sweeten it to your taste ; you must not let it boil after you put in the sor-rel, if you do it will take off the green.

You must put this sauce into a bason.

269. *To make* Almond Flummery.

Take a pint of stiff jelly made of calf's feet, put to it a jill or better of good cream, and four ounces of almonds, blanch and beat them fine with a little rose-water, then put them to your cream and jelly, let them boil together for half a quarter of an hour, and sweeten it to your taste ; strain it through a fine cloth, .and keep it stirring till it be quite cold, put it in cups and let it stand all night, loosen it in warm water and turn it out into your dish, so serve it up, and prick it with blanch'd almonds.

270. *To make* Cale's Foot Flummery.

Take two calf's feet, when they are drefs'd, put two quarts of water to them,

boil

boil them over a flow fire till half or better be confumed; when your ftock is cold, if it be too ftiff, you may put to it as much cream as jelly, boil them together with a blade or two of mace, fweeten it to your tafte with loaf-fugar, ftrain it through a fine cloth, ftir it whilft it be cold, and turn it out, but firft loofen it in warm water, and put it into your difh as you did the other flummery.

271. *To ftew* SPINAGE *with* POACHED EGGS.

Take two or three handfuls of young fpinage, pick it from the ftalks, wafh and drain it very clean, put it into a pan with a lump of butter, and a little falt, keep ftirring it all the time whilft it be enough, then take it out and fqueeze out the water, chop it and ftir in a little more butter, lie it in your difh in quarters, and betwixt every quarter a poached egg, and lie one in the middle; fry fome fippets of white bread and prick them in your fpinage, fo ferve them up.

This is proper for a fide-difh either for noon or night.

272. *To make* RATAFIA DROPS.

Take half a pound of the beft jordan almonds, and four ounces of bitter almonds, blanch and fet them before the fire to dry, beat them in a marble mortar with a little white of an egg, then put to them half a pound of powder fugar, and beat them altogether to a pretty ftiff pafte; you may beat your white of egg very well before you put it in, fo take it out, roll it with your hand

F   upon

upon a board with a little fugar, then cut
them in pieces, and lie them on fheets of
tin or paper, at equal diftances, that they
don't touch one another, and fet them in a
flow oven to bake.

273. *To fry* ARTICHOKE BOTTOMS.

Take artichoke bottoms when they are at
the full growth, and boil them as you would
do for eating, pull off the leaves, and take
out the choke, cut off the ftalks as clofe as
you can from the bottom; take two or three
eggs, beat them very well, fo dip your artichokes in them, and ftrew over them a little
pepper and falt; fry them in butter, fome
whole and fome in halves; ferve them up
with a little butter in a china cup, fet it in
the middle of your difh, lie your artichokes
round, and ferve them up.

They are proper for a fide difb either noon
or night.

274. *To fricaffee* ARTICHOKES.

Take artichokes, and order them the fame
way as you did for frying, have ready in a
ftew-pan a few morels and truffles, ftewed
in brown gravy, fo put in your artichokes,
and give them a fhake altogether in your
ftew-pan, and ferve them up hot, with fippets round them.

275. *To dry* ARTICHOKE BOTTOMS.

Take the largeft artichokes you can get,
when they are at their full growth, boil them
as you would do for eating, pull off the
leaves and take out the choke; cut off the

ftalk

ſtalk as cloſe as you can, lie them on a tin
dripping-pan, or an earthen diſh, ſet them
in a ſlow oven, for if your oven be too hot it
will brown them ; you may dry them before
the fire if you have conveniency ; when they
are dry put them in paper bags, and keep
them for uſe.

276. To ſtew APPLES.

Take a pound of double refin'd ſugar, with
a pint of water, boil and ſkim it, and put
into it a pound of the largeſt and cleareſt pippins, pared and cut in halves ; if little, let
them be whole ; core them and boil them
with a continual froth, till they be as tender
and clear as you would have them, put in the
juice of two lemons, (but firſt take out the
apples,) a little peel cut like threads, boil
down your ſirup as thick as you would have
it, then pour it over your apples ; when you
diſh them, ſtick them with long bits of candid orange, and ſome with almonds cut in
long bits, ſo ſerve them up.

You muſt ſtew them the day before you
uſe them.

277. To ſtew APPLES another way.

Take kentiſh pippins or john apples, pare
and ſlice them into fair water, ſet them on a
clear fire, and when they are boiled to maſh,
let the liquor run through a hair-ſieve ; boil
as many apples thus as will make the quantity of liquor you would have ; to a pint of
this liquor you muſt have a pound of double
refin'd loaf ſugar in great lumps, wet the

lumps

lumps of fugar with the pippin liquor, and fet it over a gentle fire, let it boil, and fkim it well ; whilft you are making the jelly, you muft have your whole pippins boiling at the fame time ; (they muft be the faireft and beft pippins you can get) fcope out the cores, and pare them neatly, put them into fair water as you do them ; you muft likewife make a fir-up ready to put them into, the quantity as you think will boil them in clear ; make the firup with double refin'd fugar and water. Tie up your whole pippins in a piece of fine cloth or muflin feverally, when your fugar and water boils put them in, let them boil very faft, fo faft that the firup always boils over them ; fometimes take them off, and then fet them on again, let them boil till they be clear and tender ; then take off the muflin they were tied up in, and put them into glaf-fes that will hold but one in a glafs ; then fee if your jelly of apple-johns be boiled to jelly enough, if it be, fqueeze in the juice of two lemons, and let it have a boil ; then ftrain it through a jelly bag into the glaffes your pippins are in ; you muft be fure that your pippins be well drained from the firup they were boiled in ; before you put them in-to the glaffes, you may, if you pleafe, boil little pieces of lemon-peel in water till they be tender, and then boil them in the firup your pippins were boiled in ; then take them out and lay them upon the pippins before the jelly is put in, and when they are cold paper them up.   278. To

278. *To make* PLUMB GRUEL.

Take half a pound of pearl barley, fet it on to cree; put to it three quarts of water; when it has boiled a while, fhift it into another frefh water. and put to it three or four blades of mace, a little lemon-peel cut in long pieces, fo let it boil whilft the barley be very foft; if it be too thick you may add a little more water; take half a pound of currants, wafh them well and plump them, and put to them your barley, half a pound of raifins and ftone them; let them boil in the gruel whilft they are plump, when they are enough put to them a little white wine, a little juice of lemon, grate in half a nutmeg, and fweeten it to your tafte, fo ferve them up.

279. *To make* RICE GRUEL.

Boil half a pound of rice in two quarts of foft water, as foft as you would have it for rice milk, with fome flices of lemon-peel, and a ftick of cinnamon; add to it a little white wine and juice of lemon to your tafte, put in a little candid orange fliced thin, and fweeten it with fine powder fugar; don't let it boil after you put in your wine and lemon, put it in a china difh, with fiye or fix flices of lemon, fo ferve it up.

280. *To make* SCOTCH CUSTARD, *to eat hot for Supper.*

Boil a quart of cream with a ftick of cinnamon, and a blade of mace; take fix eggs, both yolks and whites (leave out the ftrains) and beat them very well, grate a long bifcuit

into

into your cream, give it a boil before you put
in your eggs, mix a little of your cream a-
mongft your eggs before you put 'em in, fo
fet it over a flow fire, ftirring it about whilft
it be thick, but don't let it boil; take half a
pound of currants, wafh them very well, and
plump them, then put them to your cuftard;
you muft let your cuftard be as thick as will
bear the currants, that they don't fink to the
bottom; when you are going to difh it up,
put in a large glafs of fack, ftir it very well,
and ferve it up in a china bafon.

281. *To make a Difh of* MULL'D MILK.

Boil a quart of new milk with a ftick of
cinnamon, then put to it a pint of cream, and
let them have one boil together, take eight
eggs, (leave out half of the whites and all
the ftrains) beat them very well, put to them
a jill of milk, mix all together, and fet it over
a flow fire, ftir it whilft it begins to thicken
like cuftard, fweeten it to your tafte, and
grate in half a nutmeg; then put it into your
difh with a toaft of white bread.

This is proper for a fupper.

282. *To make* LEATCH.

Take two ounces of ifinglafs and break it
into bits, put it into hot water, then put half
a pint of new milk into the pan with the
ifinglafs, fet it on the fire to boil, and put
into it three or four fticks of good cinnamon,
two blades of mace, a nutmeg quartered, and
two or three cloves, boil it till the ifinglafs be
diffolved, run it through a hair-fieve into a
large

large pan, then put to it a quart of cream
fweetened to your tafte with loaf fugar, and
boil them a while together ; take a quarter of
a pound of blanch'd almonds beaten in rofe-
water, and ftrain out all the juice of them into the cream on the fire, and warm it, then
take it off and ftir it well together ; when it
has cooled a little take a broad fhallow difh
and put it into it through a hair-fieve, when
it is cold cut it in long pieces, and lay it a-
crofs whilft you have a pretty large difh ; fo
ferve it up.

Sometimes a lefs quantity of ifinglafs will
do, according to the goodnefs : Let it be the
whiteft and cleareft you can get.

You muft make it the day before you
want it for ufe.

283. *To make* SCOTCH OYSTERS.

Take two pounds of the thick part of a
leg of veal, cut it in little bits clear from the
fkins, and put it in a marble mortar, then
fhred a pound of beef fuet and put to it, and
beat them well together till they be as fine as
pafte ; put to it a handful of bread-crumbs
and two or three eggs, feafon it with mace,
nutmeg, pepper and falt, and work it well
together ; take one part of your forc'd-meat
and wrap it in the kell, about the bignefs of
a pigeon, the reft make into little flat cakes
and fry them ; the rolls you may either broil
in a dripping-pan, or fet them in an oven ;
three is enough in a difh, fet them in the
middle of the difb and lay the cakes round ;

F 4   then

then take fome ftrong gravy, fhred in a few
capers, and two or three mufhrooms or oyfters if you have any, fo thicken it up with a
lump of butter, and ferve it up hot. Garnifh your difh with pickles.

284. To *boil* BROCCOLI.

Take broccoli when it is feeded, or at any
other time ; take off all the low leaves of
your ftalks and tie them up in bunches as you
do afparagus, cut them the fame length you
peel your ftalks ; cut them in little pieces,
and boil them in falt and water by themfelves ; you muft let your water boil before
you put them in ; boil the heads in falt and
water, and let the water boil before you put
in the broccoli ; put in a little butter ; it
takes very little boiling, and if it boil too
quick it will take off all the heads ; you muft
drain your broccoli through a fieve as you do
afparagus ; lie the ftalks in the middle, and the
bunches round it, as you would do afparagus.

This is proper either for a fide-difb or a
middle-difb.

285. To *boil* SAVOY SPROUTS.

If your favoys be cabbag'd, drefs off the
out leaves and cut them in quarters ; take off
a little of the hard ends, and boil them in a
large quantity of water with a little falt ;
when boiled drain them, lie them round your
meat, and pour over them a little butter.

Any thing will boil greener in a large
quantity of water than otherwife.

286 To

286. *To boil* Cabbage Sprouts.

Take your sprouts, cut off the outside leaves and the hard ends, shred and boil them as you do other greens, not forgetting a little butter.

287. *To fry* Parsneps *to look like* Trout.

Take a middling sort of parsneps, not over thick, boil them as soft as you would do for eating, peel and cut them in two the long way; you must only fry the small ends, not the thick ones; beat three or four eggs, put to them a spoonful of flour, dip in your parsneps, and fry them in butter a light brown, have for your sauce a little vinegar and butter; fry some slices to lie round about the dish, and so serve them up.

288. *To make* Tansey *another Way.*

Take an old penny loaf and cut off the crust, slice it thin, put to it as much hot cream as will wet it, then put to it six eggs well beaten, a little shred lemon-peel, a little nutmeg and salt, and sweeten it to your taste; green it as you did your baked tansey; so tie it up in a cloth and boil it; (it will take an hour and a quarter boiling) when you dish it up stick it with candid orange, and lie a sevile orange cut in quarters round your dish; serve it up with a little plain butter.

289. *To make* Gooseberry Cream.

Take a quart of gooseberries, pick, coddle, and bruise them very well in a marble mortar or wooden bowl, and rub them with the back of a spoon through a hair-sieve, till you take

F 5   out

out all the pulp from the feeds; take a pint
of thick cream, mix it well among your pulp,
grate in fome lemon-peel, and fweeten it to
your tafte ; ferve it up either in a china difh
or an earthen one.

290. *To fry* Parsneps *another way.*

Boil your parfneps, cut them in pieces
about the length of your finger, dip them
in egg and a little flour, and fry them a
light brown ; when they are fried difh them
up, and grate over them a little fugar : You
muft have for the fauce a little white wine,
butter, and fugar in a bafon, and fet in the
middle of your difh.

291. *To make* Apricock Pudding.

Take ten apricocks, pare, ftone, and cut
them in two, put them into a pan with a
quarter of a pound of loaf fugar, boil them
pretty quick whilft they look clear, fo let them
ftand whilft they are cold ; then take fix
eggs, (leave out half of the whites) beat them
very well, add to them a pint of cream, mix
the cream and eggs well together with a
fpoonful of rofe-water, then put in your a-
pricocks, and beat them very well together,
with four ounces of clarified butter, then put
it into your difb with a thin pafte under it ;
half an hour will bake it.

292. *To make* Apricock Custard.

Take a pint of cream, boil it with a ftick
of cinnamon and fix eggs, (leave out four of
the whites) when your cream is a little cold,
mix your eggs and cream together, with a

quarter

quarter of a pound of fine fugar, fet it over
a flow fire, ftit it all one way whilft it begin
to be thick, then take it off and ftir it whilft
it be a little cold, and pour it into your difh;
take fix apricocks, as you did for your
pudding, rather a little higher; when they
are cold lie them upon your cuftard at
equal diftances; if it be at the time when
you have no ripe apricocks, you may lie preferv'd apricocks.

293. *To make* Jumballs *another Way.*

Take a pound of meal and dry it, a pound
of fugar finely beat, and mix thefe together;
then take the yolks of five or fix eggs, half a
jill of thick cream, or as much as will make it
up to a pafte, and fome coriander feeds, lay
them on tins and prick them; bake them in a
quick oven; before you fet them in the oven
wet them with a little rofe-water and double
refin'd fugar to ice them.

294. *To make* Peach *or* Apricock Chips.

Take a pound of chips to a pound of fugar, let not your apricocks be too ripe, pare
them and cut them into large chips; take
three quarters of a pound of fine fugar, ftrew
moft of it upon the chips, and let them ftand
till the fugar be diffolv'd, fet them on the fire,
and boil them till they are tender and clear,
ftrewing the remainder of the fugar on as they
boil, fkim them clear, and lay them in glaffes
or pots fingle, with fome firup, cover them
with double refin'd fugar, fet them in a ftove,
and when they are crifp on one fide turn the

F 6 other

ether on glaffes and parch them, then fet
them into the ftove again ; when they are
pretty dry, pour them on hair-fieves till they
are dry enough to put up.

295. *To make* Sago Gruel.

Take four ounces of fago and wafh it, fet
it over a flow fire to cree in two quarts of
fpring water, let it boil whilft it be thickifh
and foft, put in a blade or two of mace, and
a ftick of cinnamon, let it boil in a while, and
then put in a little more water ; take it off,
put to it a pint of claret, and a little candid orange ; then put in the juice of a lé-
mon, and fweeten it to your tafte ; fo ferve
it up.

296. *To make* Spinage Toasts.

Take a handful or two of young fpinage
and wafh it, drain it from the water, put it
into a pan with a lump of butter, and a little
falt, let it ftew whilft it be tender, only turn
it in the boiling, then take it up and fqueeze
out the water, put in another lump of butter and chop it fmall, put to it a handful of
currants plump'd, and a little nutmeg ; have
three toafts cut from a penny loaf well buttered, then lie on your fpinage.

This is proper for a fide-difh either at
noon or night.

297. *To roaft a* Beast Kidney.

Take a beaft kidney with a little fat on,
and ftuff it all round, feafon it with a little
pepper and falt, wrap it in a kell, and put it
upon the fpit with a little water in the dripping,

ping-pan ; what drops from your kidney thicken with a lump of butter and flour for your fauce.

To make your STUFFING.

Take a handful of fweet herbs; a few bread-crumbs, a little beef-fuet fbred fine, and two eggs, (leave out the whites) mix altogether with a little nutmeg, pepper and falt; ftuff your kidney with one part of the ftuffing, and fry the other part in little cakes; fo ferve it up.

298. To ftew CUCUMBERS.

Take middling cucumbers and cut them in flices, but not too thin, ftrew over them a little falt to bring out the water, put them into a ftew-pan or fauce-pan, with a little gravy, fome whole pepper, a lump of but-ter, and a fpoonful or two of vinegar to your tafte; let them boil all together; thicken them with flour, and ferve them up with fippets.

299. To make an OATMEAL PUDDING.

Take three or four large fpoonfuls of oat-meal done through a hair-fieve, and a pint of milk, put it into a pan and let it boil a little whilft it be thick, add to it half a pound of butter, a fpoonful of tofe-water, a little lemon-peel fhred, a little nutmeg or beaten cinnamon, and a little falt; take fix eggs, (leave out two of the whites) and put to them a quarter of a pound of fugar or better, beat them very well, fo mix them all together; put it into your difh with a pafte round your difh

edge;

edge; have a little rofe-water, butter and
fugar for fauce.

300. *To make a* CALF's HEAD PIE *another way.*

Half boil your calf's head, when it is
cold cut it in flices, rather thicker than you
would do for hafhing, feafon it with a little
mace, nutmeg, pepper and falt, then lie part of
your meat in the bottom of your pie, a few
capers, pickled oyfters, and mufhrooms; a
layer of one and a layer of another; then put
in half a pound of butter and a little gravy;
when your pie comes from the oven, have
ready the yolks of fix or eight eggs boiled
hard, and lay them round your pie; put in a
little melted butter, and a fpoonful or two of
white wine, and give them a fhake together
before you lie in your eggs; your pie mult
be a ftanding pie baked upon a difh, with a
puff-pafte round the edge of the difh, but
leave no pafte in the bottom of your pie;
when it is baked ferve it up without a lid.

This is proper for either top or bottom difh.

301. *To make* ELDER WINE.

Take twenty pounds of malaga raifins, pick
and chop them, then put them into a tub
with twenty quarts of water, let the water
be boiled and ftand till it be cold again before
you put in your raifins, let them remain together ten days, ftirring it twice a day, then
ftrain the liquor very well from the raifins,
through a canvas ftrainer or hair-fieve; add
to it fix quarts of elder juice, five pounds of
loaf fugar, and a little juice of floes to make

it acid, juft as you pleafe; put it into a veffel, and let it ftand in a pretty warm place three months, then bottle it; the veffel muft not be ftopp'd up till it has done working; if your raifins be very good you may leave out the fugar.

302. *To make* GOOSEBERRY WINE *of ripe* GOOSEBERRIES.

Pick, clean and beat your goofeberries in a marble mortar or wooden bowl, meafure them in quarts up-heap'd, add two quarts of fpring water, and let them ftand all night or twelve hours, then rub or prefs out the hufks very well; ftrain them through a wide ftrainer, and to every gallon put three pounds of fugar, and a jill of brandy, then put all into a fweet veffel, not very full, and keep it very clofe for four months, then decant it off till it comes clear, pour out the grounds, and wafh the veffel clean with a little of the wine; add to every gallon a pound more fugar, let it ftand a month in the veffel again, drop the grounds thro' a flannel bag, and put it to the other in the veffel; the tap hole muft not be over near the bottom of the cafk, for fear of letting out the grounds.

The fame receipt will ferve for currant wine the fame way; let them be red currants.

303. *To make* BALM WINE.

Take a peck of balm leaves put them in a tub or large pot, heat four gallons of water fcalding hot, ready to boil, then pour it upon the leaves, fo let it ftand all night, then ftrain them

the

them thro' a hair-fieve ; put to every gallon
of water two pounds of fine fugar, and ftir it
very well; take the whites of four or five eggs,
beat them very well, put them into a pan, and
whifk it very well before it be over-hot, when
the fkim begins to rife take it off, and keep
it fkimming all the while it is boiling, let it boil
three quarters of an hour, then put it into the
tub, when it is cold put a little new yeaft
upon it, and beat it in every two hours, that
it may head the better, fo work it for two
days, then put it into a fweet rundlet, bung
it up clofe, and when it is fine, bottle it.

304. *To make* RAISIN WINE.

Take ten gallons of water, and fifty pounds
of malaga raifins, pick out the large ftalks
and boil them in your water, when your water
is boiled, put it into a tub ; take the raifins
and chop them very fmall, when your water
is blood warm, put in your raifins, and rub
them very well with your hand ; when you
have put them into the water, let them work
for ten days, ftirting them twice a day, then
ftrain out the raifins in a hair-fieve, and put
them into a clean harden bag, and fqueeze it
in the prefs to take out the liquor, fo put it
into your barrel ; don't let it be over full,
bung it up clofe, and let it ftand whilft it is
fine ; when you tap your wine you muft not
tap it too near the bottom, for fear of the
grounds ; when it is drawn off, take the
grounds out of the barrel, and wafh it out
with a little of your wine, then put your wine

into

into the barrel again, draw your grounds thro'
a flannel bag, and put them into the barrel to
the reft; add to it two pounds of loaf fugar,
then bung it up, and let it ftand a week or
ten days; if it be very fweet to your tafte,
let it ftand fome time longer, and bottle it.

305. *To make* BIRCH WINE.

Take your birch water and boil it, clear it
with whites of eggs; to every gallon of water take two pounds and a half of fine fugar,
boil it three quarters of an hour, and when
it is almoft cold, put in a little yeaft, work it
two or three days, then put it into the barrel,
and to every five gallons put in a quart of
brandy, and half a pound of fton'd raifins;
before you put in your wine burn a brim-
ftone match in the barrel.

306. *To make* WHITE CURRANT WINE.

Take the largeft white currants you can get,
ftrip and break them in your hand, whilft you
break all the berries; to every quart of pulp
take a quart of water, let the water be boiled
and cold again, mix them well together, let
them ftand all night in your tub, then ftrain
them thro' a hair-fieve, and to every gallon
put two pounds and a half of fix-penny fugar;
when your fugar is diffolved, put it into your
barrel, diffolve a little ifinglafs, whifk it with
whites of eggs, and put it in; to every four
gallons put in a quart of mountain wine, fo
bung up your barrel; when it is fine draw it
off, and take off the grounds, (but don't tap
the barrel over low at the bottom) wafh out

the

the barrel with a little of your wine, and drop
the grounds thro' a bag, then put it to the
reft of your wine, and put it all into your barrel
again, to every gallon add half a pound more
fugar, and let it ftand another week or two;
if it be too fweet let it ftand a little longer, then
bottle it, and it will keep two or three years.

307. *To make* ORANGE ALE.

Take forty fevile oranges, pare and cut
them in flices, the beft coloured you can
get, put them all with the juice and feeds
into half a hogfhead of ale; when it is tunned
up and working, put in the oranges, and at
the fame time a pound and a half of raifins
of the fun, ftoned; when it has done working clofe up the bung, and it will be ready
to drink in a month.

308. *To make* ORANGE BRANDY.

Take a quart of brandy, the peels of eight
oranges thin pared, keep them in the brandy
forty-eight hours in a clofe pitcher, then take
three pints of water, put into it three quarters of a pound of loaf fugar, boil it till half
be confumed, and let it ftand till cold, then
mix it with the brandy.

309. *To make* ORANGE WINE.

Take fix gallons of water and fifteen pounds
of powder fugar, the whites of fix eggs well
beaten, boil them three quarters of an hour,
and fkim them while any fkim will rife; when
it is cold enough for working, put to it fix
ounces of the firup of citron or lemons,
and fix fpoonfuls of yeaft, beat the firup
and

and yeaſt well together, and put in the peel
and juice of fifty oranges, work it two days
and a night, then tun it up into a barrel, ſo
bottle it at three or four months old.

310. *To make* COWSLIP WINE.

Take ten gallons of water, when it is al-
moſt at boiling, add to it twenty one pounds
of fine powder ſugar, let it boil half an hour,
and ſkim it very clean ; when it is boiled
put it in a tub, let it ſtand till you think it
cold to ſet on the yeaſt ; take a poringer of
new yeaſt off the fat, and put to it a few
cowſlips ; when you put on the yeaſt, put
in a few every time it is ſtirred, till all the
cowſlips be in, which muſt be ſix pecks, and
let it work three or four days ; add to it ſix
lemons, cut off the peel, and the inſides put
into your barrel, then add to it a pint of
brandy ; when you think it has done working,
cloſe up your veſſel, let it ſtand a month,
and then bottle it ; you may let your cowflips he a week or ten days to dry before you
make your wine, for it makes it much finer ;
you may put in a pint of white wine that is
good, inſtead of the brandy.

311. *To make* ORANGE WINE *another way.*

Take ſix gallons of water, and fifteen
pounds of ſugar, put your ſugar into the water on the fire, the whites of ſix eggs well
beaten, and whiſk them into the water, when
it is cold ſkim it very well whilſt any ſkim
riſes, and let it boil for half an hour ; take
fifty oranges, pare them very thin, put them
into

into your tub, pour the water boiling hot
upon your oranges, and when it is blood-
warm put on the yeaft, then put in your
juice, let it work two days, and fo tun it into your barrel; at fix weeks or two months
old bottle it; you may put to it in the barrel a quart of brandy.

312. *To make* BIRCH WINE *another Way.*

To a gallon of birch water put two pounds
of loaf or very fine lump fugar, when you
put it into the pan whifk the whites of four
eggs; (four whites will ferve for four gallons) whifk them very well together before it
be boiled, when it is cold put on a little yeaft,
let it work a night and a day in the tub, before you put it into your barrel put in a brim-
ftone match burning; take two pennyworth
of ifinglafs cut in little bits, put to it a little of
your wine, let it ftand within the air of the fire
all night; take the whites of two eggs, beat
them with your ifinglafs, put them into your
barrel and ftir them about with a ftick; this
quantity will do for four gallons; to four
gallons you muft have two pounds of raifins
fhred; put them into your barrel, clofe it up,
but not too clofe at the firft, when it is fine
bottle it.

313. *To make* APRICOCK WINE.

Take twelve pounds of apricocks when full
ripe, ftone and pare them, put the parings into three gallons of water, with fix pounds of
powder fugar, boil them together half an
hour, fkim them well, and when it is blood-
warm

warm put it on the fruit; it muſt be well
bruiſed, cover it cloſe, and let it ſtand three
days; ſkim it every day as the ſkim riſes,
and put it thro' a hair-ſieve, adding a pound
of loaf ſugar; when you put it into the veſſel cloſe it up, and when it is fine bottle it.

314. *To make* ORANGE SHRUB.

Take ſevile oranges when they are full
ripe, to three dozen of oranges put half a
dozen of large lemons, pare them very thin,
the thinner the better, ſqueeze the lemons
and oranges together, ſtrain the juice thro' a
hair-ſieve, to a quart of the juice put a pound
and a quarter of loaf ſugar; about three
dozen of oranges (if they be good) will make
a quart of juice, to every quart of juice,
put a gallon of brandy, put it into a little
barrel with an open bung with all the chip-
pings of your oranges; and bung it up
cloſe; when it is fine bottle it.

This is a pleaſant dram, and ready for
punch all the year.

315. *To make* STRONG MEAD.

Take twelve gallons of water, eight pounds
of ſugar, two quarts of honey, and a few
cloves, when your pan boils take the whites
of eight or ten eggs, beat them very well,
put them into your water before it be hot,
and whiſk them very well together; do not let
it boil but ſkim it as it riſes till it has done ri-
ſing, then put it into your tub; when it is a-
bout blood warm put to it three ſpoonfuls of
new yeaſt; take eight or nine lemons, pare
them

them and fqueeze out the juice, . put them
both together into your tub, and let them
work two or three days, then put it into your
barrel, but it muft not be too full; take two
or three pennyworth of ifinglafs, cut it as
fmail as you can, beat it in a mortar about a
quarter of an hour, it will not make it fmall;
but that it may diffolve fooner, draw out a little of the mead into a quart mug, and let it
ftand within the air of the fire all night;
take the whites of three eggs, beat them very well, mix them with your ifinglafs, whifk
them together, and put them into your barrel, bung it up, and when it is fine bottle it.

You may order ifinglafs this way to put
into any fort of made wine.

316. *To make* Mead *another Way.*

Take a quart of honey, three quarts of
water, put your honey into the water, when
it is diffolved, take the whites of four or five
eggs, whifk and beat them very well together,
and put them into your pan; boil it while the
fkim rifes, and fkim it very clean; put it into
your tub, when it is warm put in two or
three fpoonfuls of light yeaft, according to
the quantity of your mead, and let it work
two nights and a day. To every gallon put
in a large lemon, pare and ftrain it, put the
juice and peel into your tub, and when it is
wrought put it into your barrel; let it work
for three or four days, ftirring it twice a day
with a thible, fo bung it up, and let it ftand
two or three months, accprding to the hot-
nefs of the weather.   You

You muſt try your mead two or three times in the above time, and if you find the ſweet-neſs going off, you muſt take it ſooner.

317. To make CYDER.

Draw off the cyder when it hath been a fortnight in the barrel, put it into the ſame barrel again when you have cleaned it from the grounds, and if your apples were ſharp, and that you find your cyder hard, put into every gallon of cyder a pound and a half of ſixpen-ny or five-penny ſugar ; to twelve gallons of this take half an ounce of iſinglaſs, and put to it a quart of cyder ; when your iſin-glaſs is diſſolved, put to it three whites of eggs, whiſk them altogether, and put them into your barrel ; keep it cloſe for two months and then bottle it.

318. To make. COWSLIP WINE.

Take two pecks of peeps, and four gal-lons of water, put to every gallon of water two pounds and a quarter of ſugar, boil the water and ſugar together a quarter of an hour, then put it into a tub to cool, put in the ſkins of four lemons, when it is cold bruiſe your peeps, and put them into your liquor, add to it a jill of yeaſt, and the juice of four lemons, let them be in the tub a night and a day, then put it into your barrel, and keep it four days, ſtirring it each day, then clay it up cloſe for three weeks and bottle it. Put a lump of ſugar in every bottle.

319. To make RED CURRANT WINE.

Let your currants be the beſt and ripeſt you

can

can get, pick and bruife them ; to every gallon of juice add five pints of water, put it
to your berries in a ftand for two nights and
a day, then ftrain your liquor through a hair-
fieve ; to every gallon of liquor put two
pounds of fugar, ftir it till it be well diffolved,
put it into a rundlet, and let it ftand four
days, then draw it off clean, put in a pound
and a half of fugar, ftirring it well, wafh out
the rundlet with fome of the liquor, fo tun
it up clofe ; if you put two or three quarts ,
of rafps bruifed among your berries, it makes
it tafte the better.

You may make white currant wine the
fame way, only leave out the rafps.

320. To make CHERRY WINE.

Take eight pounds of cherries and ftone
them, four quarts of water, and two pounds
of fugar, fkim and boil the water and fugar, then put in the cherries, let them have
one boil, put them into an earthen pot till the
next day, and fet them to drain thro' a fieve,
then put your wine into a fpigot pot, clay
it up clofe, and look at it every two or three
days after ; if it does not work, throw into it
a handful of frefh cherries, fo let it ftand fix
or eight days, then if it be clear, bottle it up.

321. To make CHERRY WINE another Way.

Take the ripeft and largeft kentifh cherries
you can get, bruife them very well, ftones
and ftalks altogether, put them into a tub,
having a tap to it, let them ftand fourteen
days, then pull out the tap, let the juice run
from

from them, and put it into a barrel, let it work three or four days, then ftop it up clofe three or four weeks and bottle it off.

This wine will keep many years and be exceeding rich.

322. *To make* LEMON DROPS.

Take a pound of loaf fugar, beat and fift it very fine, grate the rind of a lemon and put it to your fugar ; take the whites of three eggs and whifk them to a froth, fqueeze in fome lemon to your tafte, beat them for half an hour, and drop them on white paper ; be fure you let the paper be very dry, and fift a little fine fugar on the paper before you drop them. If you would have them yellow, take a pennyworth of gamboge, fteep it in fome rofe-water, mix to it fome whites of eggs and a little fugar, fo drop them, and bake them in a flow oven.

323. *To make* Goofeberry Wine *another way.*

Take twelve quarts of good ripe goofe-berries, ftamp them, and put to them twelve quarts of water, let them ftand three days, ftir them twice every day, ftrain them, and put to your liquor fourteen pounds of fugar ; when it is diffolved ftrain it through a flannel bag, and put it into a barrel, with half an ounce of ifinglafs ; you muft cut the ifinglafs in pieces, and beat it whilft it be foft, put to it a pint of your wine, and let it ftand within the air of the fire ; take the whites of four eggs and beat them very well to a froth, put in the ifinglafs, and whifk the whites and it together ; put them into the barrel, clay it

G

clofe, and let it ftand whilft fine, then bottle
it for ufe.

324. *To make* Red Currant Wine *another way.*

Take five quarts of red currants, full ripe,
bruife them, and take from them all the ftalks,
to every five quarts of fruit put a gallon of
water ; when you have your quantity, ftrain
them thro' a hair-fieve, and to every gallon
of liquor put two pounds and three quarters
of fugar ; when your fugar is diffolved tun it
into your cafk, and let it ftand three weeks,
then draw it off, and put to every gallon a
quarter of a pound of fugar ; wafh your barrel with cold water, tun it up, and let it ftand
about a week ; to every ten gallons put an
ounce of ifinglafs, diffolve it in fome of the
wine, when it is diffolved put to it a quart of
your wine, and beat them with a whifk, then
put it into the cafk, and ftop it up clofe ;
when it is fine, bottle it.

If you would have it tafte of rafps, put to e-
very gallon of wine a quart of rafps ; if there
be any grounds in the bottom of the cafk
when you draw off your wine, drop them thro'
a flannel bag, and then put it into your cafk.

325. *To make* MULBERRY WINE.

Gather your mulberries when they are full
ripe, beat them in a marble mortar, and to
every quart of berries put a quart of water ;
when you put 'em into the tub rub them very
well with your hands, and let them ftand all
night, then ftrain 'em thro' a fieve ; to every
gallon of water put three pounds of fugar,
                                          and

and when the fugar is diffolved put it into your barrel; take two pennyworth of ifinglafs and clip it in pieces, put to it a little wine, and let it ftand all night within the air of the fire; take the whites of two or three eggs, beat them very well, then put them to the ifinglafs, mix them well together, and put them into your barrel, ftirring it about when it is put in; you muft not let it be over full, nor bung it clofe up at firft; fet it in a cool place, and bottle it when fine.

326. *To make* BLACKBERRY WINE.

Take blackberries when they are full ripe, and fqueeze them the fame way as you did the mulberries. If you add a few mulherries, it will make your wine have a much better tafte.

327. *To make* SIRUP OF MULBERRIES.

Take mulberries when they are full ripe, break them very well with your hand, and drop them through a flannel bag; to every pound of juice take a pound of loaf fugar; beat it fmall, put it to your juice, fo boil and fkim it very well; you muft fkim it all the time it is boiling; when the fkim has done rifing it is enough; when it is cold bottle it and keep it for ufe.

You may make rafpberry firup the fame way.

328. *To make* RASPBERRY BRANDY.

Take a gallon of the beft brandy you can get, and gather your rafpberries when they are full ripe, and put them whole into your bran-

dy

dy; to every gallon of brandy take three quarts of rasps, let them stand close covered for a month, then clear it from the rasps, and put to it a pound of loaf sugar; when your fugar is dissolved and a little settled, bottle it and keep it for use.

329. *To make Black* CHERRY BRANDY.

Take a gallon of the best brandy, and eight pounds of black cherries, stone and put 'em into your brandy in an earthen pot; bruise the stones in a mortar, then put them into your brandy, and cover them up close, let them steep for a month or six weeks, so drain it and keep it for use.

You may distil the ingredients if you please.

330. *To make* RATAFIA BRANDY.

Take a quart of the best brandy, and about a jill of apricock kernels, blanch and bruise them in a mortar, with a spoonful or two of brandy, so put them into a large bottle with your brandy; put to it four ounces of loaf fugar, let it stand till you think it has got the taste of the kernels, then pour it out and put in a little more brandy if you please.

331. *To make* COWSLIP SIRUP.

Take a quartern of fresh pick'd cowslips, put to 'em a quart of boiling water, let 'em stand all night, and the next morning drain it from the cowslips; to every pint of water put a pound of fine powder sugar, and boil it over a slow fire; skim it all the time in the boiling whilst the skim has done rising; then take it off, and when it is cold put it into a bottle, and keep it for use.   332. *To*

332. *To make* LEMON BRANDY.

Take a gallon of brandy, chip twenty-five lemons, (let them steep twenty-four hours) the juice of sixteen lemons, a quarter of a pound of almonds blanch'd and beat, drop it thro' a jelly bag twice, and when it is fine bottle it; sweeten it to your taste with double refined sugar before you put it into your jelly bag. You must make it with the best brandy you can get.

333. *To make* CORDIAL WATER *of* COWSLIPS.

Take two quarts of cowslip peeps, a slip of balm, two sprigs of rosemary, a stick of cinnamon, half an orange peel, half a lemon peel; lay all these to steep twelve hours, in a pint of brandy, and a pint of ale; then distil them in a cold still.

334. *To make* MILK PUNCH.

Take two quarts of old milk, a quart of good brandy, the juice of six lemons or oranges, whether you please, and about six ounces of loaf-sugar, mix them altogether, and drop them thro' a jelly bag; take off the peel of two of the lemons or oranges, and put it into your bag, when it is run off bottle it; 'twill keep as long as you please.

335. *To make* MILK PUNCH *another Way*.

Take three jills of water, a jill of old milk, and a jill of brandy, sweeten it to your taste; you must not put any acid into this for it will make it curdle.

This is a cooling punch to drink in a morning.

336. To

336. *To make* PUNCH *another Way.*

Take five pints of boiling water and one quart of brandy, add to it the juice of four lemons or oranges, and about fix ounces of loaf fugar; when you have mixed it together ftrain it thro' a hair fieve or cloth, and put into your bowl the peel of a lemon or o-range.

337. *To make* ACID *for* PUNCH.

Take goofeberries at their full growth, pick and beat them in a marble mortar, and fqueeze them in a harden bag thro' a prefs, when you have done run it thro' a flannel bag, and then bottle it in fmall bottles; put a little oil on every bottle, fo keep it for ufe.

338. *To bottle* GOOSEBERRIES.

Gather your goofeberries when they are young, pick and bottle them, put in the cork loofe, fet them in a pan of water, with a little hay in the bottom, put them into the pan when the water is cold, let it ftand on a flow fire, and mind when they are coddled; don't let the pan boil, if you do it will break the bottles: when they are cold faften the cork, and put on a little rofin, fo keep them for ufe.

339. *To bottle* DAMSINS.

Take your damfins before they are full ripe, and gather them when the dew is off, pick off the ftalks, and put them into dry bottles; don't fill your bottles over full, and cork them as clofe as you would do ale, keep them in a cellar, and cover them over with fand.　　　　340. *To*

340. *To preserve Orange Chips to put in glasses.*

Take a sevile orange with a clear skin, pare it very thin from the white, then take a pair of scissars and clip it very thin, and boil it in water, shifting it two or three times in the boiling to take out the bitter; then take half a pound of double refined sugar, boil it and skim it, then put in your orange, so let it boil over a slow fire whilst your sirup be thick, and your orange look clear, then put it into glasses, and cover it with papers dipt in brandy; if you have a quantity of peel you must have the larger quantity of sugar.

341. *To preserve* ORANGES *or* LEMONS.

Take sevile oranges, the largest and roughest you can get, clear of spots, chip them very fine, and put them in water for two days, shifting them twice or three times a day, then boil them whilst they are soft; take and cut them in quarters, and take out all the pippins with a penknife, so weigh them, and to every pound of orange, take a pound and half of loaf sugar; put your sugar into a pan, and to every pound of sugar a pint of water, set it over the fire to melt, and when it boils skim it very well, then put in your oranges; if you would have any of them whole, make a little hole at the top, and take out the meat with a tea spoon, set your oranges over a slow fire to boil, and keep them skimming all the while; keep your oranges as much as you can with the skin downwards; you may cover them with a delf plate, to bear

them

them down in the boiling ; let them boil for
three quarters of an hour, then put them into a pot or bason, and let them ftand two
days covered, then boil them again whilft they
look clear, and the firup be thick, fo put
them into a pot, and lie clofe over them a
paper dip'd in brandy, and tie a double paper at the top, fet them in a cool place, and
keep them for ufe. If you would have your
oranges that are whole to look pale and clear,
to put in glaffes, you muft make a firup of
pippin jelly ; then take ten or a dozen pippins, as they are of bignefs, pare and flice
them, and boil them in as much water as will
cover them till they be thoroughly tender, fo
ftrain your water from the pippins through a
hair fieve, then ftrain it through a flannel
bag ; and to every pint of jelly take a pound
of double refined fugar, fet it over a fire to
boil, and fkim it, let it boil whilft it be thick,
then put it into a pot and cover it, but they
will keep beft if they be put every one in
different pots.

342. *To make* JELLY *of* CURRANTS.

Take a quartern of the largeft and beft
currants you can get, ftrip them from the
ftalks, and put them in a pot, ftop them clofe
up, and boil them in a pot of water over the
fire, till they be thoroughly coddled and begin
to look pale, then put them in a clear hair
fieve to drain, and run the liquor thro' a
flannel bag, to every pint of liquor put
in a pound of double refin'd fugar; you
muft

muft beat the fugar fine, and put it in by
degrees, fet it over the fire, and boil it whilft
any fkim will rife, then put it into glaffes for
ufe ; the next day clip a paper round, and
dip it in brandy to lie on your jelly ; if you
would have your jelly a light red, put in half
of white currants, and in my opinion it
looks much better.

343. *To preferve* APRICOCKS.

Take apricocks before they are full ripe,
ftone and pare 'em ; then weigh 'em, and to
every pound of apricocks take a pound of
double refined fugar, beat it very fmall, lie one
part of your fugar under the apricocks, and
the other part at the top, let them ftand all
night, the next day put them in a ftew-pan
or brafs pan ; don't do over many at once in
your pan, for fear of breaking, let them boil
over a flow fire, fkim them very well, and
turn them two or three times in the boiling ;
you muft but about half do 'em at the firft,
and let them ftand whilft they be cool, then
let them boil whilft your apricocks look clear,
and the firup thick, put them into your pots
or glaffes, when they are cold cover them
with a paper dipt in brandy, then tie another
paper clofe over your pot to keep out the
air.

344. *To make* MARMALADE *of* APRICOCKS.

Take what quantity of apricocks you fhall
think proper, ftone them and put them im-
mediately into a fkillet of boiling water, keep
them under water on the fire till they be

foft,

soft, then take them out of the water and
wipe them with a cloth, weigh your sugar
with your apricocks, weight for weight, then
dissolve your sugar in water, and boil it to a
candy height, then put in your apricocks,
being a little bruised, let them boil but a
quarter of a hour, then glass them up.

345. *To know when* SUGAR *is at* CANDY
HEIGHT.

Take some sugar and clarify it, keep it
boiling 'till it becomes thick, then stir it
with a stick from you, and when it is at
candy-height it will fly from your stick like
flakes of snow, or feathers flying in the air,
and till it comes to that height it will not
fly, then you may use it as you please.

346. *To make* Marmalade *of* Quinces *white.*

Take your quinces and coddle them as you
do apples, when they are soft pare them and
cut them in pieces, as if you would cut them
for apple pies, then put your cores, parings,
and the waste of your quinces in some water, and boil them fast for fear of turning red
until it be a strong jelly ; when you see the
jelly pretty strong strain it, and be sure you
boil them uncovered ; add as much sugar as the
weight of your quinces into your jelly, till it be
boiled to a height, then put in your coddled
quinces, and boil them uncovered till they be
enough, and set them near the fire to harden.

347. *To make* QUIDDANY *of* RED CURRANT-
BERRIES.

Put your berries into a pot, with a spoonful

or

or two of water, cover it clofe, and boil 'em
in fome water, when you think they are e-
nough ftrain them, and put to every pint of
juice a pound of loaf fugar, boil it up jelly
height, and put them into glaffes for ufe.

348. *To preferve* GOOSEBERRIES.

To a pound of fton'd goofeberries put a
pound and a quarter of fine fugar, wet the
fugar with the goofeberry jelly ; take a quart
of goofeberries, and two or three fpoonfuls
of water, boil them very quick, let your fugar be melted, and then put in your goofeberries ; boil them till clear, which will be
very quickly.

349. *To make little* ALMOND CAKES.

Take a pound of fugar and eight eggs,
beat them well an hour, then put them into
a pound of flour, beat them together, blanch
a quarter of a pound of almonds, and beat
them with rofe-water to keep 'em from oiling, mix all together, butter your tins, and
bake them half an hour.

Half an hour is rather too long for them
to ftand in the oven.

350. *To preferve* RED GOOSEBERRIES.

Take a pound of fixpenny fugar, and a little juice of currants, put to it a pound and a
half of goofeberries, and let them boil quick
a quarter of an hour ; but if they be for jam
they muft boil better than half an hour.

They are very proper for tarts, or to eat
as fweet-meats.

G 6 351. Ta

351. *To bottle* BERRIES *another Way.*

Gather your berries when they are full grown, pick and bottle them, tie a paper over them, prick it with a pin, and set it in the oven after you have drawn ; when they are coddled, take them out, and when they are cold cork them up ; rosin the cork over, and keep them for use.

352. *To keep* BARBERRIES *for* TARTS *all the Year.*

Take barberries when they are full ripe, and pick 'em from the stalk, put them into dry bottles, cork 'em up very close and keep 'em for use.

You may do cramberries the same way.

353. *To preserve* BARBERRIES *for* TARTS.

Take barberries when full ripe, strip them, take their weight in sugar, and as much water as will wet your sugar, give it a boil and skim it ; then put in your berries, let them boil whilst they look clear and your sirup thick, so put them into a pot, and when they are cold cover them up with a paper dip'd in brandy.

354. *To preserve* DAMSINS.

Take damsins before they are full ripe, and prick them, take their weight in sugar, and as much water as will wet your sugar, give it a boil and skim it, then put in your damsins, let them have one scald, and set them by whilst cold, then scald them again, and continue scalding them twice a day whilst your sirup looks thick, and the damsins clear ;

clear; you muſt never let them boil; do 'em
in a braſs pan, and do not take them out in
the doing; when they are enough put them
into a pot, and cover them up with a paper
dip'd in brandy.

355. *How to keep* DAMSINS *for* TARTS.

Take damſins before they are full ripe,
to every quart of damſins put a pound of
powder ſugar, put them into a pretty broad
pot, a layer of ſugar and a layer of damſins, tie them cloſe up, ſet them in a ſlow
oven, and let them have a heat every day
whilſt the ſirup be thick, and the damſins
enough; render a little ſheep ſuet and pour
over them, ſo keep them for uſe.

356. *To keep* DAMSINS *another Way.*

Take damſins before they be quite ripe,
pick off the ſtalks, and put them into dry
bottles; cork them as you would do ale,
and keep them in a cool place for uſe.

357. *To make* MANGO *of* CODLINS.

Take codlins when they are at their full
growth, and of the greeneſt ſort, take a little
out of the end with the ſtalk, and then take
out the core; lie them in a ſtrong ſalt and
water, let them lie ten days or more, and fill
them with the ſame ingredients as you do
other mango, only ſcald them oftner.

358. *To pickle* CURRANTBERRIES.

Take currants either red or white before
they are thoroughly ripe; you muſt not take
them from the ſtalk, make a pickle of ſalt
and

and water and a little vinegar, fo keep them
for ufe.

They are proper for garnifhing.

359. *To keep* Barberries *inſtead of preſerving.*

Take barberries and he them in a pot, a
layer of barberries and a layer of fugar, pick
the feeds out before for garnifhing fweetmeats,
if for fauces put fome vinegar to them.

360. *To keep* Afparagus *or* Green Peafe *a Year.*

Take afparagus or green peafe, green them
as you do cucumbers, and fcald them as you
do other pickles with falt and water; let it
be always new pickle, and when you would
ufe them boil them in frefh water.

361. *To make white Paſte of* PIPPINS.

Take fome pippins, pare and cut them in
halves, and take out the cores, then boil 'em
very tender in fair water, and ftrain them
thro' a fieve, then clarify two pounds of fugar
with two whites of eggs, and boil it to a candy height, put two pounds and a half of the
pulp of your pippins into it, let it ftand over
a flow fire drying, keeping it ftirring till it
comes clear from the bottom of your pan,
then lie them upon plates or boards to dry.

362. *To make green Paſte of* PIPPINS.

Take green pippins, put them into a pot
and cover them, let them ftand infufing over
a flow fire five or fix hours to draw the red-
nefs or fappinefs from them, and then ftrain
them thro' a hair fieve; take two pounds of
fugar, boil it to a candy height, put to it
two pounds of the pulp of your pippins, keep

it ſtirting over the fire till it comes clean from the bottom of your pan, then lay it on plates or boards, and ſet it in an oven or ſtove to dry.

363. To make red Paſte of PIPPINS.

Take two pounds of ſugar, clarify it, then take roſſet and temper it very well with fair water, put it into your ſirup, let it boil till your ſirup is pretty red colour'd with it, then ſtrain your ſirup thro' a fine cloth, and boil it till it be at candy-height, then put to it two pounds and a half of the pulp of pip-pins, keeping it ſtirring over the fire till it comes clean from the bottom of the pan, then lie it on plates or boards, ſo dry them.

364. To preſerve FRUIT green.

Take your fruit when they are green, and ſome fair water, ſet it on the fire, and when it is hot put in the apples, cover them cloſe, but they muſt not boil, ſo let them ſtand till they be ſoft, and there will be a thin ſkin on them, peel it off, and ſet them to cool, then put them in again, let them boil till they be very green, and keep them as whole as you can; when you think them ready to take up, make your ſirup for them; take their weight in ſugar, and when your ſirup is ready put the apples into it, and boil them very well in it; they will keep all the year near ſome fire.

You may do green plumbs or other fruit.

365. To make ORANGE MARMALADE.

Take three or four ſevile oranges, grate
them

them, take out the meat, and boil the rinds whilst they are tender; shift them three or four times in the boiling to take out the bitter, and beat them very fine in a marble mortar; to the weight of your pulp take a pound of loaf sugar, and to a pound of sugar you may add a pint of water, boil and skim it before you put in your oranges, let it boil half an hour very quick, then put in your meat, and to a pint take a pound and a half of sugar, let it boil quick half an hour, stir it all the time, and when it is boiled to a jelly, put it into pots or glasses; cover it with a paper dip'd in brandy.

366. *To make* QUINCES WHITE *another Way.*

Coddle your quinces, cut them in small pieces, and to a pound of quinces take three quarters of a pound of sugar, boil it to a candy height, having ready a quarter of a pint of quince liquor boil'd and skim'd, put the quinces and liquor to your sugar, boil them till it looks clear, which will be very quickly, then close your quince, and when cold cover it with jelly of pippins to keep the colour.

367. *To make* GOOSEBERRY VINEGAR.

To every gallon of water take six pounds of ripe gooseberries, bruise them, and pour the water boiling hot upon your berries, cover it close, and set it in a warm place to ferment, till all the berries come to the top, then draw it off, and to every gallon of liquor put a pound and a half of sugar, then tun it into a cask, set it in a warm place, and in six months it will be fit for use, 368. To

368. *To make* Goofeberry WINE *another way.*

Take three pounds of green goofeberries to a quart of water, and a pound of fugar, ftamp your berries and throw them into your water as you ftamp them, it will make them ftrain the better; when it is ftrained put in your fugar, beat it well with a difh for half an hour, than ftrain it thro' a finer ftrainer into your veffel, leaving it fome room to work, and when it is clear bottle it; your berries muft be clean pick'd before you ufe them, and let them be at their full growth when you ufe them, rather changing colour.

369. *To make* JAM OF CHERRIES.

Take ten pounds of cherries, ftone and boil them till the juice be wafted, then add to it three pounds of fugar, and give it three or four good boils, then put it into your pots.

370. *To preferve* CHERRIES.

To a pound of cherries take a pound of fugar finely fifted, with part of which ftrew the bottom of your pan, having ftoned the cherries, lay a layer of cherries and a layer of fugar, ftrewing the fugar very well over all, boil them over a quick fire a good while, keeping them clean fkim'd till they look clear, and the firup is thick and both of one colour; when you think them half done, take them off the fire for an hour, after which fet them on again, and to every pound of fruit put in a quarter of a pint of the juice of cherries and red currants, fo boil them till enough, and the firup is jellied, then put them in a pot, and keep them clofe from the air. 371. *To*

371. *To preserve* CHERRIES *for drying.*

Take two pounds of cherries and ftone
them, put to them a pound of fugar, and as
much water as will wet the fugar, then fet
them on the fire, let them boil till they
look clear, take them off the fire, and let
them ftand a while in the firup, and then
take them up and lay them on papers to dry.

372. *To preserve* FRUIT *green all the Year.*

Gather your fruit when they are three parts
ripe, on a very dry day, when the fun fhines
on them, then take earthen pots and put them
in, cover the pots with cork, or bung them
that no air can get into them, dig a place in
the earth a yard deep, fet the pots therein
and cover them with the earth very clofe,
and keep them for ufe.

When you take any out, cover them up
again, as at the firft.

373. *How to keep* KIDNEY BEANS *all Winter.*

Take kidney beans when they are young,
leave on both the ends, lay a layer of falt at
the bottom of your pot, and then a layer of
beans, and fo on till your pot be full, cover
them clofe at the top that they get no air,
and fet them in a cool place; before you boil
them lay them in water all night, let your
water boil when you put them in, (without
falt) and put into it a lump of butter about
the bignefs of a walnut.

374. *To candy* ANGELICA.

Take angelica when it is young and tender,
take off all the leaves from the ftalks, boil it
in

in the pan with some of the leaves under, and some at the top, till it be so tender that you can peel off all the skin, then put it into some water again, cover it over with some of the leaves, let it simmer over a slow fire till it be green, when it is green drain the water from it, and then weigh it; to a pound of angelica take a pound of loaf sugar, put a pint of water to every pound of sugar, boil and skim it, and then put in your angelica; it will take a great deal of boiling in the sugar, the longer you boil it and the greener it will be, boil it whilst your sugar be candy height, you may know when it is candy-height by the side of your pan; if you would have it nice and white, you must have a pound of sugar boiled candy height in a copper-dish or stew pan, set it over a chafing dish, and put into it your angelica, let it have a boil, and it will candy as you take it out.

375. To dry Pears.

Take half a peck of good baking pears, (or as many as you please) pare and put them in a pot, and to a peck of pears put in two pounds of sugar; you must put in no water but lie the parings on the top of your pears, tie them up close, and set them in a brown bread oven; when they are baked lay them in a dripping pan, and flat them a little in your pan; set them in a slow oven, and turn them every day whilst they be thoroughly dry; so keep them for use.

You may dry pippins the same way, only as you turn them grate over them a little sugar.

376. *To preserve* Currants *in bunches.*

Boil your fugar to the fourth degree of boiling, tie your currants up in bunches, then place them in order in the fugar, and give them feveral covered boilings, fkim them quick, and let them not have above two or three feethings, then fkim them again, and fet them into the ftove in the preferving pan, the next day drain them, and drefs them in bunches, ftrew them with fugar, and dry them in a ftove or in the fun.

377. *To dry* Apricocks.

To a pound of apricocks put three quarters of a pound of fugar, pare and ftone them, to a layer of fruit lie a layer of fugar, let them ftand till the next day, then boil them again till they be clear, when cold take them out of the firup, and lay them upon glaffes, or china, and fift them over with double refined fugar, fo fet them on a ftove to dry, next day if they be dry enough turn them, and fift the other fide with fugar ; let the ftones be broke and the kernels blanch'd, and give them a boil in the firup, then put them into the apricocks; you muft not do too many at a time, for fear of breaking them in the firup; do a great many, and the more you do in it, the better they will tafte.

378. *To make* Jumballs *another Way.*

Take a pound of meal dry, a pound of fugar finely beat, mix them together ; then take the yolks of five or fix eggs, as much thick cream as will make it up to a pafte,

and

and fome coriander feeds ; roll them and lay
them on tins, prick and bake them in a quick
oven ; before you fet them in the oven wet
them with a little rofe-water and double refin'd fugar, and it will ice them.

379. *To preferve* ORANGES *whole.*

Take what quantity of oranges you have
a mind to preferve, chip off the rind, the
thinner and better, put them into water twenty-four hours, in that time fhift them in the
water (to take off the bitter) three times ;
you muft fhift them with boiling water, cold
water makes them hard ; put double the
weight of fugar for oranges, diffolve your
fugar in water, fkim it, and clarify it with
the white of an egg ; before you put in your
oranges, boil them in firup three or four
times, three or four days betwixt each time ;
you muft take out the inmeat of the oranges
very clean, for fear of mudding the firup.

380. *To make* JAM *of* DAMSINS.

·Take damfins when they are ripe, and
to two pounds of damfins take a pound of
fugar, put your fugar into a pan with a jill
of water, when you have boiled it put in
your damfins, let them boil pretty quick,
fkim them all the time they are boiling,
when your firup looks thick they are enough,
put them into your pots, and when they are
cold cover them with a paper dip'd in brandy, tie them up clofe, and keep them for
ufe.

381. *To*

381. *To make clear* Cakes *of* Goofeberries.

Take a pint of jelly, a pound and a quarter of fugar, make your jelly with three or four fpoonfuls of water, and put your fugar and jelly together, fet it over the fire to heat, but don't let it boil, then put it into the cake pots, and fet it in a flow oven till iced over.

382. *To make* Bullies Cheese.

Take half a peck or a quartern of bullies, whether you pleafe, pick off the ftalks, put them in a pot, and ftop them up very clofe, fet them in a pot of water to boil for two hours, and be fure your pot be full of water, and boil them whilft they be enough, then put them in a hair-fieve to drain the liquor from the bullies ; and to every quart of liquor put a pound and a quarter of fugar, boil it over a flow fire, keeping it ftirring all the time : You may know when it is boiled high enough by the parting from the pan, put it into pots and cover it with papers dip'd in brandy, fo tie it up clofe, and keep it for ufe.

383. *To make* Jam *of* Bullies.

Take the bullies that remained in the fieve, to every quart of it take a pound of fugar, and put it to your jam, boil it over a flow fire, put it in pots, and keep it for ufe.

384. *To make* Sirup *of* Gilliflowers.

Take five pints of clipt gilliflowers, and put to them two pints of boiling water, then put them in an earthen pot to infufe a night and a day, take a ftrainer and ftrain them

out ;

out ; to a quart of your liquor put a pound and half of loaf fugar, boil it over a flow fire, and fkim it whilft any fkim rifes ; fo when it is cold bottle it for ufe.

385. *To pickle* GILLIFLOWERS.

Take clove gilliflowers, when they are at full growth, clip them and put them into a pot, put them pretty fad down, and put to them fome white wine vinegar, as much as will cover them ; fweeten them with fine powder fugar, or common loaf ; when you put in your fugar ftir them up that your fugar may go down to the bottom ; they muft be very fweet ; let them ftand two or three days, and then put in a little more vinegar ; fo tie them up for ufe.

386. *To pickle* CUCUMBERS *fliced.*

Pare thirty large cucumbers, flice them into a pewter difb, take fix onions, flice and ftrew on them fome falt, fo cover them and let them ftand to drain twenty-four hours ; make your pickle of white wine vinegar, nutmeg, pepper, cloves and mace, boil the fpices in the pickle, drain the liquor clean from the cucumbers, put them into a deep pot, pour the liquor upon them boiling hot, and cover them very clofe ; when they are cold drain the liquor from them, give it another boil, and when it is cold pour it on them again ; fo keep them for ufe.

387. *To make* CUPID HEDGE HOG's.

Take a quarter of a pound of jordan almonds, and half a pound of loaf fugar, put

it into a pan with as much water as will juft
wet it, let it boil whilft it be fo thick as will
ftick to your almonds, then put in your almonds and let them boil in it ; have ready a
quarter of a pound of fmall coloured comfits ; take your almonds out of the firup
one by one, and turn them round whilft they
be covered over, fo lie them on a pewter difb
as you do them, and fet them before the fire,
whilft you have done them all.

They are pretty to put in glaffes, or to fet
in a defert.

388. To make ALMOND HEDGE-HOGS.

Take half a pound of the beft almonds,
and blanch them, beat them with two or three
fpoonfuls of rofe-water in a marble-mortar,
very fmall, then take fix eggs, (leave out two
of the whites) beat your eggs very well, take
half a pound of loaf fugar beaten, and four
ounces of clarified butter, mix them all well
together, put them into a pan, fet them over
the fire, and keep it ftirring whilft it be ftiff,
then put it into a china-difh, and when it is
cold make it up into the fhape of an hedge-
hog, put currants for eyes, and a bit of
candid orange for tongue ; you may leave
out part of the almonds unbeaten ; take them
and fplit them in two, then cut them in long
bits to ftick into your hedge hog all over,
then take two pints of cream cuftard to pour
over your hedge hog, according to the bignefs of your difh ; lie round your difb edge
flices of candid or preferved orange, which
you have, fo ferve it up.   389. To

389. *To pot* SALMON *to keep half a Year*.

Take a fide of frefh falmon, take out the bone, cut off the head and fcale it; you muft not wafh, but wipe it with a dry cloth; cut it in three pieces, feafon it with mace, pepper, falt and nutmeg, put it into a flat pot with the fkin fide downward, lie over it a pound of butter, tie a paper over it, and fend it to the oven, about an hour and a half will bake it; if you have more falmon in your pot than three pieces it will take more baking, and you muft put in more butter; when it is baked take it out of your pot, and lie it on a fifh plate to drain, and take off the fkin, fo feafon it over again, for if it be not well fea-foned it will not keep; put it into your pot piece by piece; it will keep beft in little pots, when you put it into your pots, prefs it well down with the back of your hand, and when it is cold cover it with clarified butter, and fet it in a cool place; fo keep it for ufe.

390. *To make a* CODLIN PIE.

Take codlins before they are over old, hang them over a flow fire to codle, when they are foft peel off the fkin, fo put them into the fame water again, then cover 'em up with vine leaves, and let them hang over the fire whilft they be green; be fure you don't let them boil; lie them whole in the difh, and bake them in puff-pafte, but leave no pafte in the bottom of the difh; put to 'em a little fbred lemon-peel, a fpoonful of verjuice or juice of lemon, and as much fugar as you

H   think

think proper, according to the largenefs of
your pie.

391. *To make a* COLLIFLOWER PUDDING.

Boil the flowers in milk, take the tops
and lay them in a difh, then take three jills
of cream, the yolks of eight eggs, and the
whites of two, feafon it with nutmeg, cinnamon, mace, fugar, fack or orange-flower-
water, beat all well together, then pour it
over the colliflower, put it into the oven,
bake it as you would a cuftard, and grate fugar over it when it comes from the oven.

Take fugar, fack and butter for fauce.

392. *To make Stock for* HARTSHORN JELLY.

Take five or fix ounces of hartfhorn, put
it into a gallon of water, hang it over a flow
fire, cover it clofe, and let it boil three or
four hours, fo ftrain it ; make it the day before you ufe it, and then you may have it
ready for your jellies.

393. *To make* SIRUP OF VIOLETS.

Take violets and pick them ; to every
pound of violets put a pint of water, when
the water is juft ready to boil put it to your
violets, and ftir them well together, let them
infufe twenty four hours and ftrain them; to
every pound of firup, take almoft two
pounds of fugar, beat the fugar very well and
put it into your firup, ftir it that the fugar
may diffolve, let it ftand a day or two, ftirring it two or three times, then fet it on the
fire, let it be but warm and it will be thick
enough.

You

You may make your firup either of violets or gilliflowers, only take the weight of
fugar, let it ftand on the fire till it be very
hot, and the firup of violets muft be only
warm.

394. *To pickle* Cockles.

Take cockles at a full moon and wafh 'em,
then put them in a pan, and cover them with
a wet cloth, when they are enough put them
into a ftone bowl, take them out of the fhells
and wafh them very well in their own pickle;
let the pickle fettle every time you wafh them,
then clear it off; when you have cleaned 'em,
put the pickle into a pan, with a fpoonful or
two of white wine and a little white wine
vinegar to your tafte, put in a little Jamaica and whole pepper, boil it very well in the
pickle, then put in your cockles, let 'em have
a boil and fkim 'em, when they are cold put
them in a bottle with a little oil over them,
fet 'em in a cool place and keep 'em for ufe.

395. *To preferve Quinces whole or in quarters.*

Take the largeft quinces when they are at
full growth, pare them and throw them into
water, when you have pared them cut them
in quarters, and take out the cores ; if you
would have any whole you muft take out the
cores with a fcope ; fave all the cores and
parings, and put them in a pot or pan to
codle your quinces in, with as much water
as will cover them, fo put in your quinces in
the middle of your parings into the pan, (be
fure you cover them clofe up at the top) fo

let

let them hang over a flow fire whilft they be
thoroughly tender, then take them out and
weigh them; to every pound of quince take
a pound of loaf fugar, and to every pound
of fugar take a pint of the fame water you
codled your quinces in, fet your water and
fugar over the fire, boil it and fkim it, then
put in your quinces, and cover it clofe up,
fet it over a flow fire, and let it boil whilft
your quinces be red and the firup thick,
then put them in pots for ufe, dipping a paper in brandy to lie over them.

396. *To pickle* SHRIMPS.

Take the largeft fhrimps you can get, pick
them out of the fhells, boil them in a jill of
water, or as much water as will cover them,
according as you have a quantity of fhrimps,
ftrain them thro' a hair-fieve, then put to
the liquor a little fpice, mace, cloves, whole
pepper, white wine, white wine vinegar,
and a little falt to your tafte; boil them very
well together, when it is cold put in your
fhrimps, they are fit for ufe.

397. *To pickle* MUSCLES.

Wafh your mufcles, put them into a pan
as you do your cockles, pick them out of the
fhells, and wafh them in the liquor; be fure
you take off the beards, fo boil them in the
liquor with fpices, as you do your cockles,
only put to them a little more vinegar than
you do to cockles.

398. *To pickle* WALNUTS *green.*

Gather walnuts when they are fo young
that

that you can run a pin through them, pare them and put them in water, and let them lie four or five days, ftirring it twice a day to take out the bitter, then put them in ftrong falt and water, let them lie a week or ten days, ftir-ring it once or twice a day, then put them in frefh falt and water, and hang them over a fire, put to them a little allum, and cover them up clofe with vine leaves, let them hang over a flow fire whilft they be green, but be fure don't let them boil, when they are green put them into a lieve to drain the water from them.

399. *To make* Pickle *for them.*

Take a little good alegar, put to it a little long pepper and Jamaica pepper, a few bay leaves, a little horfe-radifh, a handful or two of muftard-feed, a little falt and a little rockambol if you have any, if not a few fha-lots; boil them altogether in the alegar, which put to your walnuts and let it ftand three or four days, giving them a fcald once a day, then tie them up for ufe.

A fpoonful of this pickle is good for fifh-fauce, or a calf's head afh.

400. *To pickle* WALNUTS *black.*

Gather walnuts when they are fo tender that you can run a pin thro' them, prick them all with a pin very well, lie them in frefh water, and let them lie for a week, fhifting them once a day; make for them a ftrong falt and water, and let them lie whilft they be yel-low, ftirring them once a day, then take 'em

H 3

out

out of the falt and water, and make a frefh
falt and water and boil it, put it on the top of
your walnuts, and let your pot ftand in the
corner end, fcald them once or twice a day
whilft they be black.

You may make the fame pickle for thofe,
as you did for the green ones.

401. *To pickle* OYSTERS.

Take the largeft oyfters you can get, pick
them whole out of the fhell, and take off the
beards, wafh them very well in their own
pickle, fo let the pickle fettle, and clear it off,
put it into a ftew-pan, put to it two or three
fpoonfuls of white wine, and a little white
wine vinegar ; don't put in any water, for
if there be not pickle enough of their own, get
a little cockle-pickle and put to it, a little Jamaica pepper, white pepper and mace, boil
and fkim them very well ; you muft fkim
it before you put in your fpices, then put in
your oyfters, and let them have a boil in the
pickle, when they are cold put them into a
large bottle, with a little oil on the top, fet
them in a cool place and keep them for ufe.

402. *To pickle large* CUCUMBERS.

Take cucumbers and put them in a ftrong
falt and water, let them lie whilft they be
throughly yellow, then fcald them in the fame
falt and water they lie in, fet them on the
fire, and fcald them once a day whilft they
are green ; take the beft alegar you can get,
put to it a little Jamaica pepper and black
pepper, fome horfe-radifh in flices, a few
bay leaves, and a little dill and falt, fo fcald

you:

your cucumbers twice or thrice in this pickle, then put them up for ufe.

403. *To pickle* ONIONS.

Take the fmalleft onions you can get, peel and put them into a large quantity of fair water, let them lie two days and fhift them twice a day; then drain them from the water, take a little diftill'd vinegar, put to 'em two or three blades of mace, and a little white pepper and falt, boil it, and pour it upon your onions, let them ftand three days, fcalding them every day, fo put them into little glaffes, and tie a bladder over them; they are very good done with alegar for common ufe, only put in Jamaica pepper inftead of mace.

404. *To pickle* ELDER BUDS.

Take elder buds when they are the bignefs of fmall walnuts, lie them in a ftrong falt and water for ten days, and then fcald them in frefh falt and water, put in a lump of allum, let them ftand in the corner end elofe cover'd up, and fcalded once a day whilft green.

You may do radifh cods or brown buds the fame way.

405. *To make the* Pickle.

Take a little alegar or white wine vinegar, and put to it two or three blades of mace, with a little whole pepper and Jamaica pepper, a few bay leaves and falt, put to your buds, and fcald them two or three times, then they are fit for ufe.

406. *To pickle* MUSHROOMS.

Take mufhrooms when frefh gather'd, fort the large ones from the buttons, cut off the

ftalks

stalks, wash them in water with a flannel, have a pan of water ready on the fire to boil 'em in, for the less they lie in the water the better; let them have two or three boils over the fire, then put them into a sieve, and when you have drained the water from them put them into a pot, throw over them a handful of salt, stop them up close with a cloth, and let them stand two or three hours on the hot hearth or range end, giving your pot a shake now and then; then drain the pickle from them, and lie them in a dry cloth for an hour or two, so put them into as much distill'd vinegar as will cover them, let them lie a week or ten days, then take them out, and put them in dry bottles; put to them a little white pepper, salt and ginger sliced, fill them up with distill'd vinegar, put over 'em a little sweet oil, and cork them up close; if your vinegar be good they will keep two or three years; I know it by experience.

You must be sure not to fill your bottles above three parts full, if you do they will not keep.

407. *To pickle* Mushrooms *another way.*

Take mushrooms and wash them with a flannel, throw them into water as you wash them, only pick the small from the large, put them into a pot, throw over them a little salt, stop up your pot close with a cloth, boil them in a pot of water as you do currants when you make a jelly, give them a shake now and then; you may guess when they are enough by the quantity of liquor that comes

from

from them; when you think they are enough
ſtrain from them the liquor, put in a little
white wine vinegar, and boil in it a little
mace, white pepper, Jamaica pepper, and
ſlic'd ginger; when it is cold put it to the
muſhrooms, bottle 'em and keep 'em for uſe.

They will keep this way very well, and
have more of the taſte of muſhrooms, but
they will not be altogether ſo white.

408. *To pickle* POTATOE CRABS.

Gather your crabs when they are young,
and about the bigneſs of a large cherry, he
them in a ſtrong ſalt and water as you do o-
ther pickles, let them ſtand for a week or
ten days, then ſcald them in the ſame water
they lie in twice a day whilſt green; make
the ſame pickle for them as you do for eu-
cumbers; be ſure you ſcald them twice or
thrice in the pickle, and they will keep the
better.

409. *To pickle large* BUTTONS.

Take your buttons, clean 'em and cut 'em
in three or four pieces, put them into a large
ſauce-pan to ſtew in their own liquor, put
to them a little Jamaica and whole pepper, a
blade or two of mace, and a little ſalt, cover
it up, let it ſtew over a ſlow fire whilſt you
think they are enough, then ſtrain from them
their liquor, and put to it a little white wine
vinegar or alegar, which you pleaſe, give it
a boil together, and when it is cold put it to
your muſhrooms, and keep them for uſe.

You may pickle flaps the ſame way.

H 5

410. *To*

410. *To make* CATCHUP.

Take large mufhrooms when they are frefh
gathered, cut off the dirty ends, break them
fmall with your hands, put them in a ftone-
bowl with a handful or two of falt, and let
them ftand all night; if you don't get mufhrooms enough at once, with a little falt they
will keep a day or two whilft you get more,
fo put 'em in a ftew-pot, and fet them in an
oven with houfhold bread; when they are
enough ftrain from 'em the liquor, and let it
ftand to fettle, then boil it with a little mace,
Jamaica and whole black pepper, two or
three fhalots, boil it over a flow fire for an
hour, when it is boiled let it ftand to fettle,
and when it is cold bottle it; if you boil it
well it will keep a year or two; you muft
put in fpices according to the quantity of
your catchup; you muft not wafh them,
nor put to them any water.

411. *To make* MANGO *of* CUCUMBERS *or*
SMALL MELONS.

Gather cucumbers when they are green,
cut a bit off the end and take out all the meat;
lie them in a ftrong falt and water, let them
lie for a week or ten days whilft they be
yellow, then fcald them in the fame falt and
water they lie in whilft green, then drain
from them the water; take a little muftard-
feed, a little horfe radifh, fome fcraped and
fome fhred fine, a handful of fhalots, a claw
or two of garlick if you like the tafte, and a
little fhred mace; take fix or eight cucumbers

bers fhred fine, mix them amongft the teft of
the ingredients, then fill your melons or cucumbers with the meat, and put in the bits
at the ends, tie them on with a ftring, fo
take as much alegar or white wine vinegar
as will well cover them, and put into it a little Jamaica and whole pepper, a little horfe-
radifh and a handful or two of muftard-feed,
then boil it, and pour it upon your mango ;
let it ftand in the corner end two or three
days, fcald them once a day, and then tie
them up for ufe.

412. To pickle GARKINS.

Take garkins of the firft growth, pick
'em clean, put 'em in a ftrong falt and water,
let 'em lie a week or ten days whilft they be
throughly yellow, then fcald them in the
fame falt and water they lie in, fcald them
once a day, and let them lie whilft they are
green, then fet them in the corner end clofe
cover'd.

413. To make Pickle for your Cucumbers.

Take a little alegar, (the quantity muft be
equal to the quantity of your cucumbers,
and fo muft your feafoning) a little pepper,
a little Jamaica and long pepper, two or
three fhalots, a little horfe-radifh fcraped
or fliced, a little falt and a bit of allum, boil
them altogether, and fcald your cucumbers
two or three times with your pickle, fo tie
them up for ufe.

414. To pickle COLLIFLOWER white.

Take the whiteft colliflower you can get,

H 6　　　　　　　　　　break

break it in pieces the bigneſs of a muſhroom;
take as much diſtill'd vinegar as will cover
it, and put to it a little white pepper, two or
three blades of mace, and a little ſalt, then
boil it and pour it on your colliflowers three
times, let it be cold, then put it into your
glaſſes or pots, and wet a bladder to tie over
it to keep out the air. You may do white
cabbage the ſame way.

415. *To pickle* RED CABBAGE.

Take a red cabbage, chuſe it a purple
red, for the light red never proves a good
colour; ſo take your cabbage and ſhred it in
very thin ſlices, ſeaſon it with pepper and
ſalt very well, let it lie all night upon a broad
tin, or a dripping-pan; take a little alegar,
put to it a little Jamaica pepper, and two or
three raſes of ginger, boil them together,
and when it is cold pour it upon your cabbage, and in two or three days time it will
be fit for uſe.

You may throw a little colliflower among
it, and it will turn red.

416. *To pickle* COLLIFLOWER *another way.*

Take the colliflower and break it in pieces
the bigneſs of a muſhroom, but leave on a
ſhort ſtalk with the head; take ſome white
wine vinegar, into a quart of vinegar, put
ſix-pennyworth of cochineal beat well, alſo a
little Jamaica and whole pepper, and a little
ſalt, boil them in vinegar, pour it over the
colliflower hot, and let it ſtand two or three
days cloſe covered up; you may ſcald it once
in three days whilſt it be red, when it is red
take

take it out of p k , and waſh the cochineal
off in the pickle, ſo ſtrain it through a hair
ſieve, and let it ſtand a little to ſettle, then
put it to your colliflower again, and tie it up
for uſe ; the longer it lies in the pickle the
redder it will be.

417. *To pickle* WALNUTS *white.*

Take walnuts when they are at full growth
and can thruſt a pin through them, the largeſt
ſort you can get, pare them, and cut a bit off
one end whilſt you ſee the white, ſo you muſt
pare off all the green, (if you cut through the
white to the kernel they will be ſpotted,) and
put them in water as you pare them ; you
muſt boil them in ſalt and water as you do
muſhrooms, they will take no more boiling
than a muſhroom ; when they are boiled lay
them on a dry cloth to drain out the water,
then put them into a pot, and put to them
as much diſtill'd vinegar as will cover them,
let them lie two or three days ; then take a
little more vinegar, put to it a few blades of
mace, a little white pepper and ſalt, boil 'em
together, when it is cold take your walnuts out
of the other pickle and put them into that, let
them lie two or three days, pour it from them,
give it another boil and ſkim it, when it is
cold put to it your walnuts again, put them
into a bottle, and put over them a little ſweet
oil, cork them up, and ſet them in a cool
place ; if your vinegar be good they will
keep as long as the muſhrooms.

418. *To pickle* BARBERRIES.

Take barberries when full ripe, put them

into

into a pot, boil a ſtrong ſalt and water, then
pour it on them boiling hot.

419. *To make* BARLEY-SUGAR.

Boil barley in water, ſtrain it through a
hair-ſieve, then put the decoction into clarified ſugar brought to a candy height, or the
laſt degree of boiling, then take it off the fire,
and let the boiling ſettle, then pour it upon
a marble ſtone rubb'd with the oil of olives,
when it cools and begins to grow hard, cut
it into pieces, and rub it into lengths as
you pleaſe.

420. *To pickle* PURSLAIN.

Take the thickeſt ſtalks of purſlain, lay
them in ſalt and water ſix weeks, then take
them out, put them into boiling water, and
cover them well ; let them hang over a ſlow
fire till they be very green, when they are
cold put them into a pot, and cover them
well with beer vinegar, and keep them covered cloſe.

421. *To make* PUNCH *another way.*

Take a quart or two of ſherbet before you
put in your brandy, and the whites of four
or five eggs, beat them very well, and ſet it
over the fire, let it have a boil, then put it
into a jelly bag, ſo mix the reſt of your acid
and brandy together, (the quantity you deſign
to make) heat it and run it all through your
jelly bag, change it in the running off whilſt
it look fine ; let the peel of one or two lemons lie in the bag ; you may make it the
day before you uſe it, and bottle it.

422. *To*

422. *To make new* COLLEGE PUDDINGS.

Grate an old penny loaf, put to it a like quantity of fuet fhred, a nutmeg grated, a little falt and fome currants, then beat fome eggs in a little fack and fugar, mix all together, and knead it as ftiff as for manchet, and make it up in the form and fize of a turkey's egg, but a little flatter; take a pound of butter, put it in a difh or ftew-pan, and fet it over a clear fire in a chafing-difh, and rub your butter about the difh till it is melted, then put your puddings in, and cover the difh, but often turn your puddings till they are brown alike, and when they are enough grate fome fugar over them, and ferve them up hot.

For a fide-difh you muft let the pafte lie for a quarter of an hour before you make up your puddings.

423. *To make a* CUSTARD PUDDING.

Take a pint of cream, mix with it fix eggs well beat, two fpoonfuls of flour, half a nutmeg grated, a little falt and fugar to your tafte; butter your cloth, put it in when the pan boils, boil it juft half an hour, and melt butter for the fauce.

424. *To make* FRYED TOASTS.

Chip a manchet very well, and cut it round ways in toafts, then take cream and eight eggs feafoned with fack, fugar, and nutmeg, and let thofe toafts fteep in it about an hour, then fry them in fweet butter, ferve them up with plain melted butter, or with butter, fack and fugar as you pleafe. 425. *To*

425. *To make* Sauce *for* Fish *or* Flesh.

Take a quart of vinegar or alegar, put it into a jug, then take Jamaica pepper whole, some sliced ginger and mace; a few cloves, some lemon-peel, horse radish sliced, sweet herbs, six shalots peeled, eight anchovies, and two or three spoonfuls of shred capers, put all those in a linen bag, and put the bag into your alegar or vinegar, stop the jug close, and keep it for use.

A spoonful cold is an addition to sauce for either fish or flesh.

426. *To make a* favoury Dish of Veal.

Cut large collops of a leg of veal, spread them abroad on a dresser, hack them with the back of a knife, and dip them in the yolks of eggs, season them with nutmeg, mace, pepper and salt, then make forc'd-meat with some of your veal, beef-suet, oysters chop'd, and sweet herbs shred fine, and the above spice, strew all these over your collops, roll and tie them up, put them on skewers, tie them to a spit and roast them; and to the rest of your forc'd meat add the yolk of an egg or two, and make it up in balls and fry them, put them in a dish with your meat when roasted, put a little water in the dish under them, and when they are enough put to it an anchovy, a little gravy, a spoonful of white wine, and thicken it up with a little flour and butter, so fry your balls and lie round the dish, and serve it up.

This is proper for a side-dish either at noon or night.

427. Ta

427. *To make* FRENCH BREAD.

Take half a peck of fine flour, the yolks of fix eggs and four whites, a little falt, a pint of ale yeaft, and as much new milk made warm as will make it a thin light pafte, ftir it about with your hand, but be fure you don't knead them; have ready fix wooden quarts or pint difhes, fill them with the pafte, (not over full) let them ftand a quarter of an hour to rife, then turn them out into the oven, and when they are baked rafp them. The oven muft be quick.

428. *To make* GINGER-BREAD *another way.*

Take three pounds of fine flour, and the rind of a lemon dried and beaten to powder, half a pound of fugar, or more if you like it, a little butter, and an ounce and a half of beaten ginger, mix all thefe together, and wet it pretty ftiff with nothing but treacle; make it into rolls or cakes which you pleafe; if you pleafe you may add candid orange peel and citron; butter your paper to bake it on, and let it be baked hard.

429. *To make* QUINCE CREAM.

Take quinces when they are full ripe, cut them in quarters, fcald them till they be foft, pare them, and mafh the clear part of them, and the pulp, and put it through a fieve, take an equal weight of quince and double refin'd fugar beaten and fifted, and the whites of eggs beat till it is as white as fnow, then put it into difhes.

You may do apple cream the fame way.

433. *To*

430. *To make* CREAM *of any preferved Fruit.*

Take half a pound of the pulp of any preferved fruit, put it in a large pan, put to it
the whites of two or three eggs, beat them
well together for an hour, then with a fpoon
take it off, and lay it heaped up high on the
difb and falver without cream, or put it in
the middle bafon.

Rafpberries will not do this way.

431. *To dry* PEARS *or* PIPPINS *without Sugar.*

Take pears or apples and wipe them clean,
take a bodkin and run it in at the head, and
out at the ftalk, put them in a flat earthen
pot and bake them, but not too much ; you
muft put a quart of ftrong new ale to half a
peck of pears, tie twice papers over the pots
that they are baked in, let them ftand till cold,
then drain them, fqueeze the pears flat, and
the apples, the eye to the ftalk, and lay 'em
on fieves with wide holes to dry, either in a
ftove or an oven not too hot.

432. *To preferve* MULBERRIES *whole.*

Set fome mulberries over the fire in a fkillet or preferving pan, draw from them a pint
of juice when it is ftrain'd ; then take three
pounds of fugar beaten very fine, wet the fugar with the pint of juice, boil up your fugar
and fkim it, put in two pounds of ripe mulberries, and let them ftand in the firup till they
are throughly warm, then fet them on the
fire, and let them boil very gently ; do them
but half enough, fo put them by in the firup
till next day, then boil them gently again ;
when

when the firup is pretty thick and will ftand in round drops when it is cold, they are e-nough, fo put all in a gally-pot for ufe.

433. To make ORANGE CAKES.

Cut your oranges, pick out the meat and juice free from the ftrings and feeds, fet it by, then boil it, and fhift the water till your peels are tender, dry them with a cloth, mince them fmall, and put them to the juice; to a pound of that weigh a pound and a half of double refin'd fugar; dip your lumps of fu-gar in water, and boil it to a candy height, take it off the fire and put in your juice and peel, ftir it well, when it is almoft cold put it into a bafon, and fet it in a ftove, then lay it thin on earthen plates to dry, and as it can-dies fafhion it with a knife, and lay them on glaffes; when your plate is empty, put more out of your bafon.

434. To dry APRICOCKS like PRUNELLOS.

Take a pound of apricocks before they be full ripe, cut them in halves or quarters, let them boil till they be very tender in a thin firup, and let them ftand a day or two in the ftove, then take them out of the firup, lay them to dry till they be as dry as prunellos, then box 'em, if you pleafe you may pare them.

You may make your firup red with the juice of red plumbs.

435. To preferve great white PLUMBS.

To a pound of white plumbs take three quarters of a pound of double refin'd fugar in lumps, dip your fugar in water, boil and

fkim

skim it very well, slit your plumbs down the seam; and put them into the sirup with the slit downwards; let them stew over the fire a quarter of an hour, skim them very well, then take them off, and when cold cover them up; turn them in the sirup two or three times a day for four or five days, then put them into pots and keep them for use.

436. *To make* Gooseberry Wine *another way.*

Take gooseberries when they are full ripe, pick and beat them in a marble mortar; to every quart of berries put a quart of water, and put them into a tub and let them stand all night, then strain them through a hair-sieve, and press them very well with your hand; to every gallon of juice put three pounds of four-penny sugar; when your sugar is melted put it into the barrel, and to as many gallons of juice as you have, take as many pounds of Malaga raisins, chop them in a bowl, and put them in the barrel with the wine; be sure let not your barrel be over full, so close it up, let it stand three months in the barrel, and when it is fine bottle it, but not before.

437. *To pickle* NASTURTIUM BUDS.

Gather your little nobs quickly after the blossoms are off, put them in cold water and salt three days, shifting them once a day; then make a pickle for them (but don't boil them at all) of some white wine, and some white wine vinegar, shalot, horse-radish, whole pepper and salt, and a blade or two of mace; then put in your seeds, and stop 'em close up. They are to be eaten as capers.

438. *To*

438. *To make* Elder-flower Wine.

Take three or four handfuls of dry'd elder-flowers, and ten gallons of spring water, boil the water, and pour it scalding hot upon the flowers, the next day put to every gallon of water five pounds of Malaga raisins, the stalks being first pick'd off, but not wash'd, chop them grosly with a chopping knife, then put them into your boiled water, stir the water, raisins and flowers well together, and do so twice a day for twelve days, then press out the juice clear as long as you can get any liquor; put it into a barrel fit for it, stop it up two or three days till it works, and in a few days stop it up close, and let it stand two or three months, then bottle it.

439. *To make* Pearl Barley Pudding.

Take half a pound of pearl barley, cree it in soft water, and shift it once or twice in the boiling till it be soft; take five eggs, put to them a pint of good cream, and half a pound of powder sugar, grate in half a nutmeg, a little salt, a spoonful or two of rose-water, and half a pound of clarified butter; when your barley is cold mix them altogether, so bake it with a puff-paste round your dish-edge.

Serve it up with a little rose-water, sugar and butter for your sauce.

440. *To make* Gooseberry Vinegar *another way*.

Take gooseberries when they are full ripe, bruise them in a marble mortar or wooden bowl, and to every upheap'd half peck of berries take a gallon of water, put it to them

in

in the barrel, let it ſtand in a warm place for two weeks, put a paper on the top of your barrel, then draw it off, waſh out the barrel, put it in again, and to every gallon add a pound of coarſe ſugar; ſet it in a warm place by the fire, and let it ſtand whilſt chriſtmas.

441. *To preſerve* APRICOCKS *green.*

Take apricocks when they are young and tender, códle them a little, rub them with a coarſe cloth to take off the ſkin, and throw them into water as you do them, and put them in the ſame water they were codled in, cover them with vine leaves, a white paper, or ſomething more at the top, the cloſer you keep them the ſooner they are green; be ſure you don't let them boil; when they are green weigh them, and to every pound of apricocks take a pound of loaf ſugar, put it into a pan, and to every pound of ſugar a jill of water, boil your ſugar and water a little, and ſkim it, then put in your apricocks, let them boil together whilſt your apricocks look clear, and your ſirup thick, ſkim it all the time it is boiling, and put them into a pot covered with a paper dip'd in brandy.

442. *To make* ORANGE CHIPS *another way.*

Pare your oranges, not over thin but narrow, throw the rinds into fair water as you pare them off, then boil them therein very faſt till they be tender, filling up the pan with boiling water as it waſtes away, then make a thin ſirup with part of the water they are boiled in, put in the rinds, and juſt let them boil,

boil, then take them off, and let them lie in the firup three or four days, then boil them again till you find the firup begin to draw between your fingers, take them off from the fire, and let them drain thro' your colander, take out but a few at a time, becaufe if they cool too faft it will be difficult to get the firup from them, which muft be done by paffing every piece of peel through your fingers, and lying them fingle on a fieve with the rind uppermoft, the fieve may be fet in a ftove, or before the fire ; but in fummer the fun is hot enough to dry them.

Three quarters of a pound of fugar will make firup to do the peels of twenty-five oranges.

443. To make Mushroom Powder.

Take about half a peck of large buttons or flaps, clean them and fet them in an earthen difh or dripping pan one by one, let them ftand in a flow oven to dry whilft they will beat to powder, and when they are powdered fift them through a fieve ; take half a quarter of an ounce of mace, and nutmeg, beat them very fine, and mix them with your mufhroom powder, then put it into a bottle, and it will be fit for ufe.

You muft not wafh your mufhrooms.

444. To preferve Apricocks another way.

Take your apricocks before they are full ripe, pare them and ftone them, and to every pound of apricocks take a pound of lump loaf-fugar, put it into you pan with as much

water

water as will wet it; to four pounds of fugar
take the whites of two eggs beat them well
to a froth, mix them well with your fugar
whilft it be cold, then fet it over the fire and
let it have a boil, take it off the fire, and put
in a fpoonful or two of water, then take off
the fkim, and do fo three or four times whilft
any fkim rifes ; put in your apricocks,
and let them have a quick boil over the fire;
take them off and turn them over, let them
ftand a little while covered, and then fet
them on again, let them have another boil and
fkim them, then take them out one by one;
fet on your firup again to boil down, and
fkim it, put in your apricocks again, and
let them boil whilft they look clear, put them
in pots, when they are cold cover them over
with a paper dipt in brandy, and tie another
paper at the top, fet them in a cool place,
and keep them for ufe.

445. *To pickle* Mushrooms *another way.*

When you have cleaned your mufhrooms
put them into a pot, throw over them a
handful of falt, ftop them very clofe with
a cloth, fet them in a pan of water to
boil about an hour, give them a fhake now
and then in the boiling, then take them out
and drain the liquor from them, wipe them
dry with a cloth, and put them up either in
white wine vinegar or diftill'd vinegar, with
fpices, and put a little oil on the top.

They don't look fo white this way, but
they have more the tafte of mufhrooms.

446 *How*

446. *How to fry* Mushrooms.

Take the largeſt and freſheſt flaps you can get, ſkin them and take out the gills, boil them in a little ſalt and water, then wipe them dry with a cloth ; take two eggs and beat them very well, half a ſpoonful of wheat-flour, and a little pepper and ſalt, then dip in your muſhrooms and fry them in butter.

They are proper to lie about ſtew'd muſh-rooms or any made diſh.

447. *How to make an* Ale Posset.

Take a quart of good milk, ſet it on the fire to boil, put in a handful or two of bread-crumbs, grate in a little nutmeg, and ſweeten it to your taſte ; take three jills of ale and give it a boil ; take the yolks of four eggs, beat them very well ; put to them a little of your ale, and mix all your ale and eggs together ; then ſet it on the fire to heat, keep ſtirring it all the time, but don't let it boil, if you do it will curdle ; then put it into your diſh, heat the milk and put it in by degrees ; ſo ſerve it up.

You may make it of any ſort of made wine ; make it half an hour before you uſe it, and keep it hot before the fire.

448. *To make* Minc'd Pies *another way.*

Take half a pound of Jordan almonds, blanch and beat them with a little roſe-water, but not over ſmall ; take a pound of beef-ſuet ſhred very fine, half a pound of apples ſhred ſmall, a pound of currants well cleaned, half a pound of powder ſugar, a little mace ſhred

I   'fine

fine, about a quarter of a pound of candid
orange cut in small pieces, a spoonful or two
of brandy, and a little salt, so mix them well
together, and bake it in a puff-paste.

449. *To make* SACK POSSET *another way.*

Take a quart of good cream, and boil it
with a blade or two of mace, put in about
a quarter of a pound of fine powder sugar;
take a pint of sack or better, set it over the
fire to heat, but don't let it boil, then grate
in a little nutmeg, and about a quarter of a
pound of powder sugar; take nine eggs,
(leave out six of the whites and strains) beat
'em very well, then put to them a little of your
sack, mix the sack and eggs very well together, then put to 'em the rest of your sack,
stir it all the time you are pouring it in, set
it over a slow fire to thicken, and stir it till it
be as thick as custard; (be sure you don't
let it boil, if you do it will curdle) then pour
it into your dish or bason; take your cream
boiling hot, and pour it to your sack by degrees, stirring it all the time you are pouring
it in, then set it on a hot hearth-stone; you
must make it half an hour before you use
it; before you set it on the hearth cover it
close with a pewter dish.

To make a FROTH *for the* POSSET.

Take a pint of the thickest cream you can
get, and beat the whites of two eggs very well,
put them to your cream, and sweeten it to
your taste, whisk them very well together,
take off the froth by spoonfuls, and lie it in
a sieve to drain; when you dish up the pos-
set lie the froth over it.   450. *To*

450. *To dry* CHERRIES *another way.*

Take cherries when full ripe, ftone them, and break 'em as little as you can in the ftoning; to fix pounds of cherries take three pounds of loaf fugar, beat it, lie one part of your fugar under your cherries, and the other at the top, let them ftand all night, then put them into your pan, and boil them pretty quick whilft your cherries change and look clear, then let them ftand in the firup all night, pour the firup from them, and put them into a pretty large fieve, and fet them either in the fun or before the fire; let them ftand to dry a little, then lay them on white papers one by one, let them ftand in the fun whilft they be thoroughly dry; in the drying turn them over, then put them into a little box; betwixt every layer of cherries lie a paper, and fo do till all are in, then lie a paper at the top, and keep them for ufe.

You muft not boil them over long in the firup,. for if it be over thick it will keep them from drying; you may boil two or three pounds more cherries in the firup after.

451. *How to order* STURGEON.

If your fturgeon be alive, keep it a night and a day before you ufe it; then cut off the head and tail, fplit it down the back, and cut it into as many pieces as you pleafe; falt it with bay falt and common falt, as you would do beef for hanging, and let it lie 24 hours; then tie it up very tight, and boil it in falt

and

and water .whilft it is tender ; (you muft not boil it over much) when it is boiled throw over it a little falt, and fet it by till it be cold. Take the head and fplit it in two, and tye it up very tight ; you muft boil it by itfelf, not fo much as you did the reft, but falt it after the fame manner.

452. *To make the* PICKLE.

Take a gallon of foft water, and make it into a ftrong brine ; take a gallon of ftale beer, and a gallon of the beft vinegar, and let all boil together, with a few fpices ; when it is cold put in your fturgeon ; you may keep it (if clofe covered) three or four months before you need to renew the pickle.

453. *To make* HOTCH-POTCH.

Take five or fix pounds of frefh beef, put it into a kettle with fix quarts of foft water, and an onion ; fet it on a flow fire, and let it boil till your beef is almoft enough ; then put in the fcrag of a neck of mutton, and let them boil together till the broth be very good ; put in two or three handfuls of bread-crumbs, two or three carrots and turnips cut fmall, (but boil the carrots in water before you put them in, elfe they will give your broth a tafte) with half a peck of fhill'd peafe, but take up the meat before you put them in, when you put in the peafe take the other part of your mutton and cut it in chops, (for it will take no more boiling than the peafe) and put it in with a few fweet herbs fhred very fmall, and falt to your tafte.

You

You must send up the mutton chops in the dish with the hotch-potch.

When there are no peafe to be had, you may put in the heads of afparagus, and if there be neither of thefe to be had, you may shred in a green favoy cabbage.

This is a proper dish inftead of foop.

454. *To make* MINC'D COLLOPS.

Take two or three pounds of any tender part of beef, (according as you would have the dish in bignefs) cut it fmall as you would do minc'd veal; take an onion, shred it fmall, and fry it a light brown in bu..r feafoned with nutmeg, pepper and falt, and put the meat into your pan with your onion, and fry it a little whilft it be a light brown; then put to it a jill of good gravy, and a fpoonful of walnut pickle, or a little catchup; put in a few shred capers or mushrooms, thicken it up with a little flour and butter; if you pleafe you may put in a little juice of lemon; when you dish it up, garnish your dish with pickle, and a few forc'd-meat balls.

It is proper for either fide-dish or top-dish.

455. *To make white* Scotch Collops *another way*

Take two pounds of the folid part of a leg of veal, cut in pretty thin flices, and feafon it with a little shred mace and falt, put it into your ftew-pan with a lump of butter, fet it over the fire, keep it ftirring all the time, but don't let it boil; when you are going to dish up the collops, put to them the yolks of two or three eggs, three fpoonfuls

I 3 of

of cream, a fpoonful or two of white wine, and a little juice of lemon, fhake it over the fire whilft it be fo thick that the fauce fticks to the meat, be fure you don't let it boil.

Garnifh your difh with lemon and fippets, and ferve it up hot.

This is proper for either fide-difh or top-difh, noon or hight.

456. *To make* VINEGAR *another way.*

Take as many gallons of water as you pleafe, and to every gallon of water put in a pound of four-penny fugar, boil it for half an hour and fkim it all the time; when it is about blood warm put to it about three or four fpoonfuls of light yeaft, let it work in the tub a night and a day, put it into your veffel, clofe up the top with a paper, and fet it as near the fire as you have convenience, and in two or three days it will be good vinegar.

457. *To preferve* QUINCES *another way.*

Take quinces, pare and put them into water, fave all the parings and cores, let 'em lie in the water with the quinces, fet them over the fire with the parings and cores to codle, cover them clofe up at the top with the parings, and lie over them either a difh-cover or pewter difh, and cover them clofe; let them hang over a very flow fire whilft they be tender; but don't let them boil; when they are foft take them out of the water, and weigh your quinces, and to every pound put a pint of the fame water they were codled in (when ftrained) and a pound of fugar; put

t em

them into a pot or pewter flaggon, the pewter makes them a much better colour; clofe
them up with a little coarfe pafte, and fet
them in a bread oven all night; if the firup
be too thin boil it down, put it to your
quinces, and keep it for ufe.

You may either do it with powder fugar
or loaf-fugar.

458. *To make* Almond Cheefecakes *another way*

Take the peel of two or three lemons
pared thick, boil them pretty foft, and change
the water two or three times in the boiling;
when they are boiled beat them very fine with
a little loaf fugar, then take eight eggs,
(leaving out fix of the whites) half a pound
of loaf or powder fugar, beat the eggs and
fugar for half an hour, or better; take a
quarter of a pound of the beft almonds,
blanch and beat them with three or four
fpoonfuls of rofe-water, but not over fmall;
take ten ounces of frefh butter, melt it without water, and clear off from it the butter-
milk, then mix them altogether very well,
and bake them in a flow oven in a puff-pafte;
before you put them into the tins, put in
the juice of half a lemon.

When you put them in the oven grate
over them a little loaf fugar.

You may make them without almonds, if
you pleafe.

You may make a pudding of the fame,
only leave out the almonds.

F I N I S.

English Housewifery *improved*;

OR, A

SUPPLEMENT

TO

MOXON's COOKERY.

CONTAINING

Upwards of Sixty Modern and Valuable

RECEIPTS

IN

| PASTRY, | MADE DISHES, |
| PRESERVING, | MADE WINES, *&c. &c.* |

Collected by a PERSON of JUDGMENT.

With CORRECTIONS and ADDITIONS.

The THIRD EDITION.

L E E D S :

Printed by GRIFFITH WRIGHT,
For GEORGE COPPERTHWAITE, Bookseller,
M,DCC,LXIX.

A

SUPPLEMENT

TO

MOXON's Cookery.

1. *A* GRANADE.

TAKE the caul of a leg of veal, lie it into a round pot; put a layer of the flitch part of bacon at the bottom, then a layer of forc'd-meat, and a layer of the leg part of veal cut as for collops, 'till the pot is fill'd up; which done, take the part of the caul that lies over the edge of the pot, clofe it up, tie a paper over, and fend it to the oven; when baked, turn it out into your difh,——*Sauce.* A good light brown gravy, with a few mufhrooms, morels, or truffles: ferve it up hot.

2. *The*

2. *The fine Brown* JELLY.

Boil four calf's feet in fix quarts of water 'till it is reduced to three pints, take off the feet and let the ftock cool, then melt it, and have ready in a ftew-pan, a fpoonful of butter hot, add to it a fpoonful of fine flour, ftir it with a wood fpoon over a ftove-fire, 'till it is very brown, but not burnt, then put the jelly out, and let it boil; when cold take off the fat, melt the jelly again, and put to it half a pint of red port, the juice and peel of half a lemon, white pepper, mace, a little Jamaica pepper, and a little falt; then have ready the whites of four eggs, well froth'd, and put them into the jelly, (take care the jelly be not too hot when the whites are put in) ftir it well together, and boil it over a quick fire one minute, run it thro' a flannel bag and turn it back till it is clear, and what form you would have it, have that ready, pour a little of the jelly in the bottom, it will foon ftarken; then place what you pleafe in it, either pigeon or fmall chicken, fweet-bread larded, or pickled fmelt or trout, place them in order, and pour on the remainder of the jelly. You may fend it up in this form, or turn it into another difh, with holding it over hot water; but not till it is thoroughly hardened.

3. *To make a* MELON.

Make the leaneft forc'd-meat that you can, green it as near the colour of melon as poffible

fible with the juice of fpinage, as little of
the juice as you can; put feveral herbs in it,
efpecially parfley fhred fine, for that will
help to green it; roll it an inch and a half
thick, lay one half in a large melon mould,
well buttered and floured, with the other half
the full fize of the mould, fides and all; then
put into it as many ftew'd oyfters as will near
fill it with liquor fufficient to keep them moift,
and clofe the forc'd-meat well together; clofe
the melon and boil till you think it is e-
nough; then make a fmall hole (if poffible
,not to be perceived) pour in a little more of
the liquor that the oyfters were ftew'd in hot,
and ferve it up with hot fauce in the difh.
It muft be boiled in a cloth, and is either for
a firft or fecond courfe.

4. *Hot* CHICKEN PIE.

Order the chickens as for fricaffee, and
forni the pie deep, lay in the bottom a mince-
meat made of the chicken's livers, ham,
parfley and yolks of eggs, feafon with white
pepper, mace, and a little falt; moiften with
butter, then lay the chicken above the mine'd
meat, and a little more butter; cover the pie
and bake it two hours; when baked take off
the fat, and add to it white gravy, with a little juice of lemon. Serve this up hot.

5. SHEEP's RUMPS *with* Rice.

Stew the rumps very tender, then take 'em
out to cool, dip them in egg and bread-
crumbs, and fry them a light brown; have

I 6   ready

ready half a pound of rice, well wash'd and pick'd, and half a pound of butter; let it ftew ten minutes in a little pot; then add a pint of good gravy to the rice and butter, and let it ftew half an hour longer; have ready fix onions boil'd very tender, and fix yolks of boil'd eggs, ftick them with cloves; then place the fheep rumps on the difh, and put round them the rice as neatly as you can; place the onions and eggs over the rice, fo ferve it up hot.

6. Sheep's Tongues *broiled.*

The tongues being boil'd, put a lump of butter in a ftew-pan, with parfley and green onions cut fmall; then fplit the tongues, but do not part them, and put them in the pan; feafon them with pepper, herbs, mace, and nutmeg; fet them a moment on the fire, and ftrew crumbs of bread on them; let them be broil'd and difh them up, with a high gravy fauce.

7. *To lard* Oysters.

Make a ftrong effence of ham and veal, with a little mace; then lard the large oyfters with a find larding pin; put them, with as much effence as will cover them, into a ftew-pan; let them ftew an hour, or more, over a flow fire. They are ufed for garnifhing, but when you make a difh of them, fqueeze in a fevile orange.

8. Veal Couley.

Take a little lean bacon and veal, onion, and

and the yellow part of a carrot, put it into a ftew-pan; fet it over a flow fire, and let it fimmer till the gravy is quite brown, then put in fmall gravy, or boiling water; boil it a quarter of an hour, and then it is ready for ufe. Take two necks of mutton, bone them, lard one with bacon, the other with parfley; when larded, put a little couley over a flow ftove, with a flice of lemon whilft the mutton is fet, then fkewer it up like a couple of rabbits, put it on the fpit and roaft it as you would any other mutton; then ferve it up with ragoo'd cucumbers. This will do for firft courfe; bottom difh.

9. *The* Mock Turtle.

Take a fine large calf's head, cleans'd well and ftew'd very tender, a leg of veal twelve pounds weight, leave out three pounds of the fineft part of it; then take three fine large fowls, (bone them, but leave the meat as whole as poffible) and four pounds of the fineft ham fliced; then boil the veal, fowls bones, and the ham in fix quarts of water, till it is reduced to two quarts, put in the fowl and the three pounds of veal, and let them boil half an hour; take it off the fire and ftrain the gravy from it; add 'to the gravy three pints of the beft white wine, boil it up and thicken it; then put in the calf's-head; have in readinefs twelve large forc'd meat balls, as large as an egg, and twelve yolks of eggs boil'd haid. Difh it up hot in a terreen.

10. *To*

10. *To dress* Ox Lips.

Take three or four ox lips, boil them as tender as poſſible, dreſs them clean the day before they are uſed; then make a rich forc'd-meat of chicken or half-roaſted rabbits, and ſtuff the lips with it; they will naturally turn round; tie them up with pack-thread and put them into gravy to ſtew; they muſt ſtew while the forc'd-meat be enough. Serve them up with truffles, morels, muſhrooms, cockſ-combs, forc'd-meat balls, and a little lemon to your taſte.

This is a top-diſh for ſecond, or ſide diſh for firſt courſe.

11. *To make* POVERADE.

Take a pint of good gravy, half a jill of elder vinegar, ſix ſhalots, a little pepper and ſalt, boil all theſe together a few minutes, and ſtrain it off. This is a proper ſauce for turkey, or any other ſort of white fowls.

12. *To pot* PARTRIDGES.

Take the partridges and ſeaſon them well with mace, ſalt and a little pepper; lie 'em in the pot with the breaſt downwards, to every partridge put three quarters of a pound of butter, ſend them to the oven; when baked, drain them from the butter and gravy, and add a little more ſeaſoning, then put them cloſe in the pot with the breaſts upwards, and when cold, cover them well with the butter, ſute the pot to the number of the partridges to have it full. You may pot any ſort of moor game the ſame way.

13. To

13. *To pot* PARTRIDGES *another way.*

Put a little thyme and parfley in the infide of the partridges, feafon them with mace, pepper and falt ; put them in the pot, and cover them with butter ; when baked, take out the partridges, and pick all the meat from the bones, lie the meat in a pot (without beating) fkim all the butter from the gravy, and cover the pot well with the butter.

14. *To pot* CHAR.

Scrape and gut them, wafh and dry them clean, feafon them with pepper, falt, mace, and nutmeg ; let the two laft feafonings be higher than the other ; put a little butter at the bottom of the pot ; then lie in the fifh, and put butter at the top, three pounds of butter to four pounds of char ; when they are baked (before they are cold) pour off the gravy and butter, put two or three fpoonfuls of butter into the pot you keep them in, then lie in the fifh ; fkim the butter clean from the gravy, and put the butter over the fifh, fo keep it for ufe.

15. SALMON *en* Maigre.

Cut fome flices of frefh falmon the thicknefs of your thumb, put them in a ftew-pan with a little onion, white pepper and mace, and a bunch of fweet herbs, pour over it half a pint of white wine, half a jill of water, and four ounces of butter (to a pound and half of falmon ;) cover the ftew-pan clofe; and ftew it half an hour ; then take out the
falmon

salmon and place it on the difh ; ftrain off the
liquor, and have ready craw-fifh, pick'd
from the fhell, or lobfter cut in fmall pieces ;
pound the fhells of the craw-fifh, or the feeds
of the lobfter, and give it a turn in the liquor ; thicken it, and ferve it up hot with the
craw-fifh, or lobfter, over the falmon.

Trouts may be done the fame way, only
cut off their heads.

16. Lobster A'L'Italienne.

Cut the tail of the lobfter in fquare pieces,
take the meat out of the claws, bruife the red
part of the lobfter very fine, ftir it in a pan
with a little butter, put fome gravy to it ;
ftrain it off while hot, then put in the lobfter with a little falt ; make it hot, and fend
it up with fippets round your difh.

17. To do Chickens or any Fowl's Feet.

Scald the feet till the fkin will come off,
then cut off the nails ; ftew them in a pot
clofe cover'd fet in water, and fome pieces of
fat meat till they are very tender ; when you
fet them on the fire, put to them fome whole
pepper, onions, falt, and fome fweet herbs ;
when they are taken out, wet them over with
the yolk of an egg, and dredge them well
with bread-crumbs ; fo fry them crifp.

18. Larks done in Jelly.

Boil a knuckle of veal in a gallon of water
till it is reduced to three pints, (it muft not
be covered but done over a clear fire) fkim
it well and clarify it, then feafon the larks
with

with pepper and falt, put them in a pot with butter, and fend them to the oven; when baked take them out of the butter whilft hot, take the jelly and feafon it to your tafte with pepper and falt; then put the jelly and larks into a pan together, and give them a fcald over the fire; fo lie them in pots and cover them well with jelly. When you would ufe them, turn them out of the pots, and ferve them up.

19. *The fine* CATCHUP.

Take three quarts of red port, a pint of vinegar, one pound of anchovies unwafh'd, pickle and all together, half an ounce of mace, ten cloves, eight races of ginger, one fpoonful of black pepper, eight ounces of horferaddifh, half a lemon-peel, a bunch of winterfavory, and four fhalots; ftew thefe in a pot, within a kettle of water, one full hour, then ftrain it thro' a clofe fieve, and when it is cold bottle it; fhake it well before you bottle it, that the fediment may mix. You may ftew all the ingredients over again, in a quart of wine for prefent ufe.

20. WALNUT CATCHUP.

Take the walnuts when they are ready for pickling, beat them in a mortar, and ftrain the juice thro' a flannel bag; put to a quart of juice a jill of white wine, a jill of vinegar, twelve fhalots fliced, a quarter of an ounce of mace, two nutmegs fliced, one ounce of black pepper, twenty four cloves,

and

and the peels of two fevile oranges, pared fo
thin that no white appears, boil it over a flow
fire very well, and fkim it as it boils; let it
ftand a week or ten days cover'd very clofe,
then pour it thro' the bag, and bottle it.

21. *A very good* White *or* Almond Soop.

Take veal, fowl, or any white meat, boiled down with a little mace, (or other fpice
to your tafte) let thefe boil to mafh, then
ftrain off the gravy ; take fome of the white
flefhy part of the meat and rub it thro' a colander ; have ready two ounces of almonds
beat fine, rub thefe thro' the colander, then
put all into the gravy, fet it on the fire to
thicken a little, and ftir in it two or three
fpoonfuls of cream, and a little butter work'd
in flour; then have ready a French roll cr·fp'd
for the middle, and flips of bread cut long
like Savoy bifcuits. Serve it up hot.

22. ALMOND PUDDING.

Take one pound of almonds, blanch'd and
beat fine, one pint of cream, the yolks of
twelve eggs, two ounces of grated bread,
half a pound of fuet, marrow, or melted
butter, three quarters of a pound of fine fugar, a little lemon-peel and cinnamon ; bake
it in a flow oven, in a difh, or little tins.
The above are very good put in fkins.

23. ALMOND PUDDING *another way*.

Boil a quart of cream, when cold, mix in
the whites of feven eggs well beat ; blanch
five ounces of almonds, beat them with rofe
or

or orange-flower water, mix in the eggs and cream; fweeten it to your tafte with fine powder fugar, then mix in a little citron or orange, put a thin pafte at the bottom, and a thicker round the edge of the difh. Bake it in a flow oven.——Sauce. Wine and fugar.

24. ALMOND CHEESECAKES *another way.*

Six ounces of almonds, blanch'd and beat with rofe-water; fix ounces of butter beat to cream; half a pound of fine fugar; fix eggs well beat, and a little mace. Bake thefe in little tins, in cold butter pafte.

25. *A* LEMON PUDDING *another way.*

Take a quarter of a pound of almonds, three quarters of a pound of fugar, beat and fearc'd, half a pound of butter; beat the almonds with a little rofe-water, grate the rinds of two lemons, beat eleven eggs, leave out two whites, melt the butter and ftir it in; when the oven is ready mix all thefe well together, with the juice of one or two lemons to your tafte; put a thin pafte at the bottom, and a thicker round the edge of the difh.

Sauce. Wine and fugar.

26. POTATOE PUDDING *another way.*

Take three quarters of a pound of potatoes, when boil'd and peel'd, beat them in a mortar with a quarter of a pound of fuet or butter, (if butter, melt it) a quarter of a pound of powder fugar, five eggs well beat, a pint of good milk, one fpoonful of flour, a little mace or cinnamon, and three fpoonfuls of

wine

wine or brandy ; mix all thefe well together, and bake it in a pretty quick oven.

Sauce. Wine and butter.

27. CARROT PUDDING *another way.*

Take half a pound of carrots, when boil'd and peel'd, beat them in a mortar, two ounces of grated bread, a pint of cream, half a pound of fuet or marrow, a glafs of fack, a little cinnamon, half a pound of fugar, fix eggs well beat, leaving out three of the whites, and a quarter of a pound of macaroons ; mix all well together ; puff-pafte round the difh-edge.——Sauce. Wine and fugar.

28. WHITE POTT *another way.*

A layer of white bread cut thin at the bottom of the difb, a layer of apples cut thin, a layer of marrow or fuet, currants, raifins, fugar and nutmeg, then the bread, and fo on, as above, till the difh is fill'd up ; beat four eggs, and mix them with a pint of good milk, a little fugar and nutmeg, and pour it over the top. This fhould be made three or four hours before it is baked.

Sauee. Wine and butter.

29. HUNTING PUDDING *another way.*

Take a pound of grated bread, a pound of fuet and a pound of currants, eight eggs, a glafs of brandy, a little fugar, and a little beat cinnamon ; mix thefe well together, and boil it two hours at the leaft.

30. ALMOND BISCUITS.

Blanch a pound of almonds, lie them in

water

water for three or four hours, dry them with
a cloth, and beat them fine with eight fpoonfuls of rofe or orange-flower water ; then
boil a pound of fine fugar to wire-height,
and ftir in the almonds, mix them well over
the fire ; but do not let them boil ; pour
them into a bafon, and beat them with a
fpoon 'till quite cold ; then beat fix whites
of eggs, a quarter of a pound of ftarch,
beat and fearc'd, beat the eggs and ftarch
together, 'till thick ; ftir in the almonds,
and put them in queen-cake tins, half full,
duft them over with a little fearc'd fugar ;
bake 'em in a flow oven, and keep them dry.

31. *To make* ALMOND BUTTER *another way.*

Take a quart of cream, fix eggs well
beat, mix them and ftrain them into a pan,
keep it ftirring on the fire whilft it be ready
to boil ; then add a jack of fack, keeping
it ftirring till it comes to a curd ; wrap it
clofe in a cloth till the whey be run from it ;
then put the curd into a mortar, and beat it
very fine, together with a quarter of a pound
of blanch'd almonds, beaten with rofe-water, and half a pound of loaf fugar : When
all thefe are well beaten together, put it into
glaffes.

This will keep a fortnight.

32. APRICOCK JUMBALLS.

Take ripe apricocks, pare, ftone, and beat
them fmall, then boil them till they are thick,
and the moifture dry'd up, then take them

off

off the fire, and beat them up with searc'd
sugar, to make them into pretty stiff paste,
roll them, without sugar, the thickness of
a straw; make them up in little knots in
what form you please; dry them in a stove
or in the sun. You may make jumballs of
any sort of fruit the same way.

33. BURNT CREAM.

Boil a stick of cinnamon in a pint of cream,
four eggs well beat, leaving out two whites,
boil the cream and thicken it with the eggs
as for a custard; then put it in your dish,
and put over it half a pound of loaf sugar
beat and seare'd; heat a fire-shovel red-hot,
and hold it over the top till the sugar be
brown. So serve it up.

34. *Little* PLUMB CAKES.

Take two pounds of flour dry'd, three
pounds of currants well wash'd, pick'd and
dry'd, four eggs beaten with two spoonfuls
of sack, half a jack of cream, and one
spoonful of orange-flower or rose-water;
two nutmegs grated, one pound of butter
wash'd in rose-water and rub'd into the flour,
and one pound of loaf sugar searc'd, mix all
well together, and put in the currants; butter
the tins and bake them in a quick oven:
half an hour will bake them.

35. York GINGER-BREAD *another way.*

Take two pounds and a half of stale bread
grated fine, (but not dry'd) two pounds of fine
powder sugar, an ounce of cinnamon, half

an.

an ounce of mace, half an ounce of ginger, a quarter of an ounce of faunders, and a quarter of a pound of almonds ; boil the fugar, faunders, ginger, and mace in half a a pint of red wine ; then put in three fpoonfuls of brandy, cinnamon, and a quarter of an ounce of cloves ; ftir in half the bread on the fire, but do not let it boil ; pour it put, and work in the reft of the bread with the almonds ; then fmother it clofe half an hour ; print it with cinnamon and fugar fearc'd, and keep it dry.

36. GINGER-BREAD *in little Tins.*

To three quarters of a pound of flour, put half a pound of treacle, one pound of fugar, and a quarter of a pound of butter ; mace, cloves, and nutmeg, in all a quarter of an ounce ; a little ginger, and a few caraway feeds ; melt the butter in a glafs of brandy, mix altogether with one egg ; then butter the tins, and bake them in a pretty quick oven.

37. OAT-MEAL CAKES.

Take a peck of fine flour, half a peck of oat-meal, and mix it well together ; put to it feven eggs well beat, three quarts of new milk, a little warm water, a pint of fack, and a pint of new yeaft ; mix all thefe well together, and let it ftand to rife ; then bake them. Butter the ftone every time you lie on the cakes, and make them rather thicker than a pan-cake.

38. BATH

38. Bath Cakes.

Take two pounds of flour, a pound of sugar, and a pound of butter; wash the butter in orange-flower water, and dry the flour; rub the butter into the flour as for puff-paste, beat three eggs fine in three spoonfuls of cream, and a little mace and salt; mix these well together with your hand, and make them into little flat cakes; rub them over with white of egg, and grate sugar upon them; a quarter of an hour will bake them in a slow oven.

39. *A Rich White* Plumb-Cake.

Take four pounds of flour dry'd, two pounds of butter, one pound and a half of double refin'd sugar beat and seare'd, beat the butter to a cream, then put in the sugar and beat it well together; sixteen eggs leaving out four yolks; a pint of new yeast; five jills of good cream, and one ounce of mace shred; beat the eggs well, and mix them with the butter and sugar; put the mace in the flour; warm the cream, mix it with the yeast, and run it thro' a hair-sieve, mix all these into a paste; then add one pound of almonds blanch'd and cut small, and six pounds of currants well wash'd, pick'd and dry'd; when the oven is ready, stir in the currants, with one pound of citron, lemon or orange; then butter the hoop and put it in.

This cake will require two hours and a half baking in a quick oven.

K

40. *An*

40. *An* Ising *for the* Cake.

One pound and a half of double-refin'd
sugar, beat and searc'd; the whites of four
eggs, the bigness of a walnut of gum-dragon steep'd in rose or orange-flower water; two ounces of starch, beat fine with a
little powder-blue; (which adds to the white-
ness) while the cake is baking, beat the ising,
and lie it on with a knife as soon as the cake
is brought from the oven.

41. Lemon Brandy.

Pour a gallon of brandy into an earthen
pot, put to it the yellow peel of two dozen
lemons, let it stand two days and two
nights, then pour two quarts of spring water
into a pan and diffolve in it two pounds of
refin'd loaf sugar, boil it a quarter of an hour,
and put it to the brandy; then boil and skim
three jills of blue milk, and mix all together,
let it stand two days more, then run it thro'
a flannel bag, or a paper within a funnel,
and bottle it.

42. *To make* Ratafia *another way.*

Take a hundred apricock stones, break
them, and bruise the kernels, then put them
in a quart of the best brandy; let them stand
a fortnight; shake them every day; put to
them fix ounces of white sugar-candy, and
let them stand a week longer; then put the
liquor thro' a jelly bag, and bottle it for use.

43. *To preserve* Grapes *all Winter.*

Pull them when dry, dip the stalks about
an inch in boiling water, and seal the end
with

with wax; chop wheat ſtraw and put a lit
tle at the bottom of a barrel, then a layer
of grapes, and a layer of ſtraw, 'till the
barrel is fill'd up; do not lie the bunches
too near one another; ſtop the barrel cloſe,
and ſet it in a dry place; but not any way
in the ſun.

44. To preſerve Grapes another way.

Take ripe grapes and ſtone them; to every
pound of grapes take a pound of double-refined ſugar; let them ſtand till the ſugar is
diſſolved; boil them pretty quick till clear;
then ſtrain out the grapes, and add half a
pound of pippin jelly, and half a pound more
ſugar; boil and ſkim it till it comes to a
jelly; put in the grapes to heat; afterwards
ſtrain them out, and give the jelly a boil;
put it to the grapes, and ſtir it till near cold;
then glaſs it.

45. Barberry Cakes.

Draw off the juice as for currant jelly,
take the weight of the jelly in ſugar, boil
the ſugar to ſugar again; put in the jelly,
and keep it ſtirring till the ſugar is diſſolved; let it be hot, but not boil; pour it out,
and ſtir it three or four times; when it is
near cold drop it on glaſſes in little cakes,
and ſet them in the ſtove. If you would
have them in the form of jumballs, boil the
ſugar to a high candy, but not to ſugar a-
gain, and pour it on a pie-plate; when it will
part from the plate cut it, and turn them into what form you pleaſe.

46. Bar-

46. BARBERRY DROPS.

When the barberries are full ripe, pull 'em off the ftalk, put them in a pot, and boil them in a pan of water till they are foft; pulp them thro' a hair-fieve; beat and fearce the fugar, and mix as much of the fearc'd fugar with the pulp, as will make it of the confiftance of a light pafte; then drop them with a pen-knife on paper (glaz'd with a flight ftone) and fet them within the air of the fire for an hour, then take them off the paper and keep them dry.

47. *To candy* ORANGES *whole another way.*

Take fevile oranges, pare off the rinds as thin as you can; tie them in a thin cloth (with a lead weight to keep the cloth down) put 'em in a lead or ciftern of river water; let them lie five or fix days, ftirring 'em about every day, then boil them while they are fo tender that you may put a ftraw thro' them; mark them at the top with a thimble, cut it out, and take out all the infide very carefully, then wafh the fkins clean in warm water, and fet them to drain with the tops downwards; fine the fugar very well, and when it is cold put in the oranges; drain the firup from the oranges, and boil it every day till it be very thick, then once a month; one orange will take a pound of fugar.

48. *To candy* GINGER.

Take the thickeft races of ginger, put
them

them in an earthen pot, and cover them with river water; put frefh water to them every day for a fortnight; then tie the ginger in a cloth, and boil it an hour in a large pan of water; fcrape off the brown rind, and cut the infide of the races as broad and thin as you can, one pound of ginger will take three pounds of loaf fugar; beat and fearce the fugar, and put a layer of the thin-flic'd ginger, and a layer of fearc'd fugar into an earthen bowl, having fugar at the top; ftir it well every other day for a fortnight, then boil it over a little charcoal; when it is candy-height take it out of the pan as quick as you can with a fpoon, and lie it in cakes on a board; when near cold take them off and keep them dry.

49. *To preferve* WINE-SOURS.

Take wine-fours and loaf-fugar an equal weight, wet the fugar with water; the white of one egg will fine four pounds of fugar, and as the fkim rifes throw on a little water; then take off the pan, let it ftand a little to fettle and fkim it; boil it again while any fkim rifes; when it is clear and a thick firup, take it off, and let it ftand till near cold; then nick the plumbs down the feam, and let them have a gentle heat over the fire; take the plumbs and firup and let them ftand a day or two, but don't cover them; then give them another gentle heat; let them ftand a day longer, and heat them again; take the plumbs

K 3

out and drain them, boil the firup and fkim it well; put it on the wine-fours, and when cold, put them into bottles or pots, tie a bladder clofe over the top, fo keep them for ufe.

50. CURRANT JELLY.

Take eight pounds of ripe, pick'd fruit, put thefe into three pounds of fugar boil'd candy-height, and fo let thefe fimmer till the jelly will fet; then run it off clear thro' a flannel bag, and glafs it up for ufe. This never looks blue, nor fkims half fo much, as the other way.

51. *To preferve red or white* CURRANTS *whole.*

Pick two pounds of currants from the ftalks, then take a pound and a half of loaf fugar, and wet it in half a pint of currant juice, put in the berries, and boil them over a flow fire till they are clear; when cold put them in fmall berry bottles, with a little mutton fuet over them.

52. SIRUP OF POPPIES.

Take two pounds of poppy flowers, two ounces of raifins, fbred them, and to every pound of poppies put a quart of boiling wa-ter, half an ounce of fliced liquorice, and a quarter of an ounce of annifeeds; let thefe ftand twelve hours to infufe, then ftrain off the liquor, and put it upon the fame quan-tity of poppies, raifins, liquorice, and an-nifeeds as before, and let this ftand twelve hours to infufe, which muft be in a pitcher

fet

set within a pot or pan of hot water; then strain it, and take the weight in sugar, and boil it to a sirup: when it is cold, bottle it.

53. *To make* BLACK PAPER *for drawing Patterns.*

Take a quarter of a pound of mutton suet, and one ounce of bees wax, melt both together, and put in as much lamp black as will colour it dark enough, then spread it over your paper with a rag, and hold it to the fire to make it smooth.

54. GOOSEBERRY VINEGAR *another way.*

To every gallon of water, put six pounds of ripe gooseberries; boil the water and let it be cold, squeeze the berries, and then pour on the water; let it stand cover'd three days pretty warm to work, stirring it once a day; then strain it off, and to every six gallons put three pounds of coarse sugar, let it stand till it has done working, then bung it up, and keep it moderately warm; in nine months it will be ready for use.

55. *To make bad ale into good strong Beer.*

Draw off the ale into a clean vessel, (suppose half a hogshead) only leave out eight or ten quarts, to which put four pounds of good hops, boil this near an hour; when quite cold, put the ale and hops into the hogshead, with eight pounds of treacle, mix'd well with four or five quarts of boil'd ale; stir it well together, and bung it up close: Let it stand six months, then bottle it for use.

56. *Green*

56. *Green* Gooseberry Wine.

To every quart of gooseberries, take a quart of spring water, bruise them in a mortar, put the water to them and let them stand two or three days; strain it off, and to every gallon of liquor put three pounds and a half of sugar; put it into a barrel, and it will of itself rise to a froth, which take off, and keep the barrel full; when the froth is all work'd off, bung it up for six weeks, then rack it off, and when the lees are clean taken out, put the wine into the same barrel again; to every gallon put half a pound of sugar, made into sirup, and when cold mix it with the wine; to every five gallons, have an ounce of isinglass, dissolv'd in a little of the wine, and put in with the sirup, so bung it up; when fine, you may either bottle it or draw it out of the vessel. Lisbon sugar is thought the best. This wine drinks like sack.

57. Ginger Wine.

Take fourteen quarts of water, three pounds of loaf sugar, and one ounce of ginger sliced thin, boil these together half an hour, fine it with the whites of two eggs; when new milk warm put in three lemons, a quart of brandy, and a white bread toast covered on both sides with yeast; put all these together into a stand, and work it one day; then tun it: It will be ready to bottle in five days, and ready to drink in a week after it is bottled.

58. Cow=

58. Cowslip Wine *another way*.

To five gallons of water, put two pecks of cowflip peeps, and thirteen pounds of loaf fugar; boil the fugar and water with the rinds of two lemons half an hour, and fine it with the whites of two eggs; when it is near cold put in the cowflips, and fet on fix fpoonfuls of new yeaft, work it two days, ftirring it twice a day; when you fqueeze out the peeps to tun it, put in the juice of fix lemons, and when it has done working in the veffel, put in a quarter of an ounce of ifinglafs diffolv'd in a little of the wine till it is a jelly; add a pint of brandy, bung it clofe up two months, then bottle it. This is right good.

59. Strong Mead *another way*.

To thirty quarts of water, put ten quarts of honey, let the water be pretty warm, then break in the honey, ftirring it till it be all diffolv'd; boil it a full half hour, when clean fkim'd that no more will rife, put in half an ounce of hops, pick'd clean from the ftalks; a quarter of an ounce of ginger fliced (only put in half the ginger) and boil it a quarter of an hour longer; then lade it out into the ftand thro' a hair-tems, and put the remainder of the ginger in, when it is cold tun it into the veffel, which muft be full, but not clay'd up till near a month: make it the latter end of *September*, and keep it a year in the veffel after it is clayed up.

K 5   60. French

60. French Bread.

To half a peck of flour, put a full jill of
new yeaft, and a little falt, make it with new
milk (warmer than from the cow) firft put
the flour and barm together, then pour in
the milk, make it a little ftiffer than a feed-
cake, duft it and your hands well with flour,
pull it in little pieces, and mould it with flour
very quick ; put it in the difhes, and cover
them with a warm cloth (if the weather re-
quires it) and let them rife till they are half
up, then fet them in the oven, (not in the
difhes, but turn them with the tops down
upon the peel ;) when baked rafp them.

61. *The fine* Rush Cheese.

Take one quart of cream, and put to it
a gallon of new milk, pretty warm, adding
a good fpoonful of earning ; ftir in a little
falt, and fet it before the fire till it be cum'd ;
then put it into a vat in a cloth ; after a day
and night turn it out of the vat into a rufh
box nine inches in length and five in breadth.
The rufhes muft be wafh'd every time the
cheefe is turn'd.

62. *To make* Raspberry Jam.

Bruife a pint of rafpberries in a little currant juice, add to it one pound and a quarter of loaf-fugar beat fine, boil it over a
flow fire, ftirring it till it jellies, then pour
it into your pots, and when cold, put on
papers dip'd in brandy, and tie other papers
over them.

63. *To make* STOUGHTON.

Take fix drams of cochineal beat fine, a quarter of an ounce of faffron three drams of rhubarb one ounce of gentian cut fmall, and the parings of five or fix fevile oranges ; to thefe ingredients put three pints of brandy, let all ftand within the air of the fire three or four days : then pour off the liquor, and fill the bottle again with brandy, putting in the peel of one or two oranges : Let this ftand fix or eight days, then pour it off thro' a fine cloth ; mix the former and this toge-ther, and it is fit for ufe.

64. *To make* ORANGE BUTTER.

Take a quarter of an ounce of clear o-range juice, and a quarter of a pint of white wine ; fteep the peel of an orange in it a-bout half an hour, take it out, and put in as much fugar as will take off the fharpnefs ; beat the yolks of fix eggs very well, mix them with it, and fet it upon the fire, ftir-ring it continually till it is almoft as thick as butter ; juft before you take it off ftir in the bignefs of a nut of butter. Make it the day before you ufe it, and ferve it up as other butter.

65. *To make a* SAGO PUDDING *another way.*

Take two ounces of fago, boil it pretty foft in three jills of new milk, with a little mace or cinnamon ; when it is cold put in four ounces of beef fuet, two ounces of grated bread, two fpoonfuls of brandy or

K 6 · wine,

wine, four ounces of fugar, and a little nutmeg, candid lemon, orange or citron.

66. *To make* COWSLIP WINE *another way.*

Take eight gallons of water, add to it
twenty pounds of loaf or fine powder fugar,
and the whites of five or fix eggs; boil it half
an hour, and fkim it very clean; pour it into a tub, and when it is blood warm put in
eight pecks of peeps, the parings and juice
of eight lemons, and fet on fourteen fpoonfuls of new yeaft; work it four or five days,
ftirring it every day; fqueefe out the peeps,
tun it, and put in a little ifinglafs infufed
in a quart of brandy; bung it up clofe three
weeks, then bottle it off: put a lump of
fugar into each bottle.

67. *To make* WAFER BISCUITS.

Take nine eggs beat, and one pound of
loaf-fugar powder'd, beat them well together till they be very white and ftiff; add
half a pound of fine flour, and a few caraway feeds, and mix all very well; drop them
on papers oil'd with warm butter; round
them; grate a little refin'd fugar over them,
and fet them in the oven: when they are
half baked take them off the papers with a
long knife, and bend them on poles which
have been warm'd in the oven; fet them in
the oven again, bake them pretty crifp, and
let them ftand on the poles till they are cold.

68. *To make* GINGER-BREAD *for keeping.*

Take two pounds of dried flour, a pound
and half of treacle, one pound of five-pen-
ny-

ny fugar, half an ounce of race-ginger beat
and lifted, a half-pennyworth of caraway-
feeds, and a large glafs of brandy ; mix all
well together, make it into little cakes, and
bake 'em on a dripping-pan : half an hour
will bake 'em in a brifk oven. Thefe will
keep years.

69. *To make* GINGER LOZENGES.

Beat and fearce one ounce of race-ginger,
put one pound of loaf-fugar in a pan, with
as much water as will wet it ; when this boils
mix your ginger well in it, and boil it candy
height ; drop it in little cakes on a fieve,
and keep 'em dry for ufe.

70. *To make a* SCALDED PUDDING.

Take four fpoonfuls of flour, pour upon
it one pint of boiling milk, ftirring it all the
time that you pour on the milk; when cold
beat a little falt with four eggs, mix all well
together : one hour will boil it. This eats
like bread pudding. You may add fruit.

71. *To make a* SCALDED PUDDING *another way.*

Beat four eggs and a little falt, mix in as
much flour as the eggs will wet ; when well
beaten, pour in one pint of hot milk. One
hour will boil it. This eats like cuftard.

72. *To make* SAUSAGES.

Take a loyn of mutton, cut and fhred it
fmail, feafon it to your tafte with pepper,
falt, a little nutmeg, and a little dried fage ;
beat three eggs with a little water, and mix
all well together ; fo fill the fkins for ufe.

73. *To*

73. To make PORTABLE SOOP.

Take a leg of veal and an old cock, skin the cock, and take all the fat from that and the veal, put to them twelve or fourteen quarts of water, a very little whole white pepper and mace, but no salt; (you must skim your pot exceeding well before you put in the spices) let all these boil together till the meat is quite a mash, the water wasted to about three pints or two quarts, and the liquor exceeding strong; when you think it is enough strain it into a stone-bowl thro' a pretty fine hair-sieve, let it stand all night, then clear off all the top and bottom as you do calf's foot jelly, and boil the pure part of the liquor till it be so strong a jelly, that when it is cold, the fire will harden, and not melt it; when you think it enough pour it into tea-cups, about two table-spoonfuls in a cup; let it stand all night; the next morning turn out the little cakes upon a pewter dish, and set them before the fire; if they run you must boil them higher; if they dry they are enough: You must keep them, in a paper bag, where there is a fire, as damp will dissolve them.

N. B. The first boiling should be in an iron-pot; the second in a clean scoured brass-pan.

74. To make HASTY CURDS.

Set on the fire one gallon of well water, and when it boils put in a little salt; in which mix well one quart of good cream
and

and eight eggs well beat; (if you add a
fpoonful or two of four cream, it will make
'em crack the fooner) let the pan ftand on
the fire while the curds rife, then put 'em
into a cloth over a fieve, tie and hang 'em
up. When well drain'd, they are ready for
ufe.

75. *To Dry* PEARS *another way.*

Take ftone pears and pare them, leaving the ftalk on, lay them in a dripping-
pan, and fet them in an oven till they are
baked pretty foft; then prefs 'em with a
fpoon, and lay 'em on a pewter-difh, grate
fome loaf-fugar very thick on them, and fet
'em before the fire, or in the fun to dry;
turn them, and grate fugar on the other fide,
and keep them in a dry place for ufe.

76. *To make the* GOLD WATER.

Take two quarts of the beft brandy, one
pound of loaf-fugar, half an ounce of fpirits
of faffron, half a dram of the oil of cloves,
and a dram of alkermes; put all thefe into a
large bottle, fhake them well together, then
take four or five leaves of gold; grind 'em
with a little loaf-fugar, and put into it a little ambergris ftop it clofe, and fet it in a
place moderately warm for three or four
days, then pour off the clear into bottles,
and cork 'em faft down; fo keep it for ufe.

77. *To make a* CALF's-FOOT PUDDING
another way.

Boil two calf's-feet, fhred them fmall, with
half a pound of beef-fuet; take a ftale penny
loaf

loaf grated, half a pound of currants, half
a nutmeg, a little mace, and four eggs well
beaten, beat all thefe very well together, and
put to 'em half a poringer of cream ; let it
boil one hour and half ; then take it out of
the cloth, and ftick in a few blanch'd almonds. Make your fauce of thick butter,
a glafs of white wine, and a little fugar.
78. To candy Lemons or Oranges another
way.

Lay the oranges in clear foft water for fix
days, fhifting them every day, pare or grate
the out-fide off very thin ; to fix fkins put a
pan full of water ; let them boil till they be
fo tender that a ftraw will go through them ;
take half a pound of loaf-fugar, put to it
as much water as will cover the fkins, give
'em a boil up, and let 'em lay in that five or
fix days longer ; then fet them on the fire
with the firup, and boil them till they be
well hot through ; lay them on a fieve before
the fire to dry ; cut them in two, and take
carefully out the infide, without breaking
the rind ; wipe them very dry, and lay
them on a fieve again ; put one pound of
loaf-fugar into a pan, and as much water as
will juft melt the fugar ; fet it over the fire,
and let it fimmer eafily till it begin to be
thick ; then put in the fkins one by one,
and let 'em fimmer till your fugar be thin
again ; keep 'em ftill fimmering till the fugar ftick to them, and be of a candy height ;
then take 'em out with a fork, and lay them
over

over a fieve before the fire. Ufe double
refin'd fugar.

79. *To make* PUNCH *for keeping.*

Take the parings of feven lemons, and
as many oranges pared thin, fteep them in
a quart of brandy clofe cork'd, in a large
berry bottle, for, twenty-four hours; then
to fix quarts of water put two pounds of
loaf-fugar clarified, let it boil a quarter
of an hour and fkim it; let it ftand till
'tis cold; ftrain the brandy from the parings, and mix it and three quarts more with
the fugar and water, and add the juice of
the lemons and oranges; put it in a veffel
proper for the quantity; ftop it very clofe,
and in three months you may bottle it. If
the lemons are large, only ufe fix. This
will keep years.

F I N I S.

A
BILL of FARE
FOR
EVERY SEASON of the YEAR.

For *J A N U A R Y*
First C
T the Top ʒvy Soop.
Remove Fiſh.
At the Bottom a Ham.
In the Middle ſtew'd Oyſters or Brawn.
For the four Corners,
A Fricaſſee of Rabbits, Scotch Col-
lops, boil'd Chickens, Calf-Foot Pie, or Oyſter
Loaves.

Second Courſe.
At the Top Wild Ducks.
At the Bottom a Turkey.
In the Middle Jellies or Lemon Poſſet.
For the four Corners,
Lobſters and Tarts, Cream Curds, ſtew'd Pears or
preſerv'd Quinces.

For *F E B R U A R Y.*
Firſt Courſe.
At the Top a Soop remove.
At the Bottom Salmon or ſtew'd Breaſt of Veal.
For the four Corners,
A Couple of Fowls with Oyſter Sauce, Pudding,
Mutton Cutlets, a Fricaſſee of Pigs Ears.

Second

Second Courſe.

At the Top Partridges.

At the Bottom a Couple of Ducks.

For the four Corners,

Stew'd Apples, preſerv'd Quinces, Cuſtards, Almond Cheeſe Cakes.

In the Middle Jellies.

For *M A R C H.*

Firſt Courſe.

At the Top a boil'd Turkey, with Oyſter Sauce.

At the Bottom a couple of roaſt Tongues or roaſt Beef.

In the Middle Pickles.

Two Side-diſhes, a Pigeon Pie and a Calf-head Haſh.

For the four Corners,

Stew'd Crab or Oyſters, Hunters Pudding, a brown Fricaſſee, ſtew'd Eels, or broil'd Whitings.

Seco d Courſe

At the Top Woodcocks or Wild Ducks.

At the Bottom Pig or Hare.

In the Middle Jellies or Sweetmeats.

For the four Corners,

Raſpberry Cream, Tarts, ſtew'd Apples, and preſerv'd Apricocks.

For *A P R I L.*

Firſt Courſe.

At the Top ſtew'd Fillet of Veal.

At the Bottom a roaſt Leg of Mutton.

Two Side-diſhes, Salt-Fiſh and Beef Steaks.

In the Middle a Hunters Pudding.

Second Courſe.

At the Top roaſt Chickens and Aſparagus.

At the Bottom Ducks.

In the Middle preſerv'd Oranges.

For the four Corners,

Damſin Pie, Cream Curds, Lobſter, and cold Pot.

For *M A Y.*

Firſt Courſe.

At the Top ſtew'd Carp or Tench.

At the Bottom a ſtew'd Rump of Beef.

In the Middle a Sallet.

For

A BILL of FARE,

For the four Corners,
A Fricaſſee of Tripes, boil'd Chickens, a Pudding, Olives of Veal.

Second Courſe.
At the Top Rabbits or Turkey Pouts.
At the Bottom green Gooſe or young Ducks.
For the four Corners,
Lemon Cream, Quince Cream, Tarts, Almond Cuſtards.
In the Middle Jellies.

For *J U N E.*

Firſt Courſe.
At the Top roaſt Pike.
At the Bottom Scotch Collops.
In the Middle ſtew'd Crab.
For the four Corners,
Boil'd Chickens, Quaking-Pudding, roaſt Tongue with Veniſon Sauce, Beans and Bacon.

Second Courſe.
At the Top a Turkey
At the Bottom Ducks or Rabbits.
In the Middle Strawberries
Two Side-diſhes, roaſt Lobſter and Peaſe.
For the four Corners,
Green Codlings, Apricock Cuſtard. Sweetmeat-Tarts, preſerv'd Damſins, or Flummery.

For *J U L Y.*

Firſt Courſe.
At the Top green Peaſe Soop, remove ſtew'd Breaſt of Veal white
At the Bottom a Haunch of Veniſon.
In the Middle a Pudding.
Two Side-diſhes, a Diſh of Fiſh, and a Fricaſſee of Rabbits.

Second Courſe.
At the Top Partridges or Pheaſants.
At the Bottom Ducks or Turkey.
In the Middle a Diſh of Fruit.
For the four Corners,
Solomon Gundie, Lobſter, Tarts, Chocolate Cream.

For

For every SEASON of the YEAR.

For *A U G U S T.*

Firſt Courſe.

At the Top Fiſh.

At the Bottom Veniſon Paſty.

In the Middle Herb Dumplings.

For the four Corners.

Fricaſſee of Rabbits, ſtew'd Pigeons, boil'd Chickens.
Fricaſſee of Veal Sweetbreads with Artichoke Bottoms.

Second Courſe.

At the Top Pheaſants or Partridges.

At the Bottom wild Ducks or Teal.

In the Middle Jellies or Syllabubs.

For the four Corners,

Preſerv'd Apricocks, Almond Cheeſe cakes, Cuſtards, and Sturgeon.

For *S E P T E M B E R.*

Firſt Courſe.

At the Top collar'd Calf-Head, with ſtew'd Pallets, Veal Sweetbreads, and forc'd Meat-Balls.

At the Bottom Udder and Tongue, or a Haunch of Veniſon.

In the Middle an Amblet of Cockles, or roaſt Lobſter.

Two Side-diſhes, Pigeon Pie and boil'd Chickens.

Second Courſe.

At the Top a roaſt Pheaſant.

At the Bottom a Turkey.

For the four Corners,

Partridges, Artichoke Bottoms fry'd, Oyſter Loaves and Teal.

For *O C T O B E R.*

Firſt Courſe.

At the Top ſtew'd Tench and Cod's Head.

At the Bottom roaſt Pork or a Gooſe.

Two Side-diſhes, roaſt Fiſh, and boil'd Fowl and Bacon.

For the four Corners,

Jug'd Pigeons, Mutton Collops, Beef Rolls, and Veal Sweetbreads fricaſſee'd.

In the Middle minc'd Pies or Oyſter Loaves.

Second Courſe.

At the Top Wild Fowl.   At

A Bill of Fare,

At the Bottom a Hare.

In the Middle Jellies.

Two Side-dishes, roasted Lobster and fry'd Cream.

For the four Corners,

Preserv'd Quinces, or stew'd Pears, Sturgeon, cold Tongue, and Orange Cheese-cakes.

For NOVEMBER.

First Course.

At the Top a Dish of Fish.

At the Bottom a Turkey Pie.

Two Side-dishes, Scotch Collops, and boil'd Tongue with Sprouts.

In the Middle scallop'd Oysters.

Second Course.

At the Top a Dish of Wild Fowl.

At the Bottom roast Lobster.

In the Middle Lemon Cream.

For the four Corners,

Tarts, Curds, Apricocks, and Solomon Gundie.

For DECEMBER.

First Course.

At the Bottom boil'd Fowls.

Two Side-dishes, Bacon and Greens, and a Dish of Scotch Collops.

In the Middle minc'd Pies or Pudding.

Second Course.

At the Top a Turkey.

In the Middle hot Apple-Pie.

For the four Corners,

Custard, Raspberry Cream, cold Pot and Crabs.

✳✳✳✳✳✳✳✳✳✳✳✳✳✳✳✳✳✳✳✳✳✳✳

A Supper for January.

AT the Top a Dish of Plumb Gruel.

Remove, boil'd Fowls.

At the Bottom a Dish of Scotch Collops·

In the Middle Jellies.

For the four Corners,

Lobster, Solomon Gundie, Custard, Tarts.　　For

For *F E B R U A R Y.*

At the Top a Dish of Fish.
Remove, a Couple of roasted Fowls.
At the Bottom Wild Ducks.

For the four Corners,
Collar'd Pig, Cheese cakes, stew'd Apples and Curds.
In the Middle hot minc'd Pies.

For *M A R C H.*

At the Top a Sack Posset.
Remove, a Couple of Ducks.
At the Bottom a boil'd Turkey, with Oyster Sauce.
In the Middle Lemon Posset.
Two Side-dishes, roasted Lobster, Oyster Pie.

For the four Corners,
Almond Custards, Flummery, Cheese-Cakes, and stew'd Apples.

For *A P R I L.*

At the Top boil'd Chickens.
At the Bottom a Breast of Veal.
In the Middle Jellies.

For the four Corners,
Orange Pudding, Custards, Tarts, and stew'd Oysters.

For *M A Y.*

At the Top a Dish of Fish.
At the Bottom Lamb or Mutton Steakes.
In the Middle Lemon Cream or Jellies.
Two Side-dishes, Tarts, Raspberry Cream.

For the four Corners,
Veal Sweetbreads, stew'd Spinage, with poach'd Eggs and Bacon, Oysters in scallop'd Shells, boil'd Chickens.

For *J U N E.*

At the Top boil'd Chickens.
At the Bottom a Tongue.
In the Middle Lemon Posset.

For the four Corners,
Cream Curds or Custards, potted Ducks, Tarts, Lobsters, Artichokes or Pease.

For *J U L Y.*

At the Top Scotch Collops.
At the Bottom roast Chickens.
In the Middle stew'd Mushrooms.   For

A BILL of FARE, &c.

For the four Corners.

Cuſtards, Lobſters, ſplit Tongue, and Solomon Gundie.

For *A U G U S T.*

At the Top ſtew'd Breaſt of Veal.

At the Bottom roaſt Turkey.

In the Middle Pickles or Fruit.

For the four Corners.

Cheeſe-Cakes and Flummery, preſerv'd Apricocks, preſerv'd Quinces.

For *S E P T E M B E R.*

At the Top boil'd Chickens.

At the Bottom a carbonaded Breaſt of Mutton, with Caper Sauce.

In the Middle Oyſters in ſcallop Shells, or ſtew'd Oyſters.

Two Side-diſhes, hot Apple-Pie and Cuſtard.

For *O C T O B E R.*

At the Top Rice Gruel

Remove, a Couple of Ducks.

At the Bottom a boil'd Turkey, with Oyſter Sauce.

In the Middle Jellies.

For the four Corners,

Lobſter or Crab, Black Caps, Cuſtard or Cream, Tarts or collar'd Pig.

For *N O V E M B E R.*

At the Top Fiſh.

At the Bottom Ducks or Teal.

In the Middle Oyſter Loaves.

Remove, a Diſh of Fruit

Two Side-diſhes, minc'd Pies, Mutton Steaks with Muſhrooms and Balls.

For *D E C E M B E R.*

At the Top boil'd Chickens.

At the Bottom a Diſh of Scotch Collops or Veal Cutlets

In the Middle Brawn.

Remove, Tarts.

For the four Corners,

Boil'd Whitings or fry'd Soles, new College Puddings, Bologna Sauſages, Scotch Cuſtard.   A

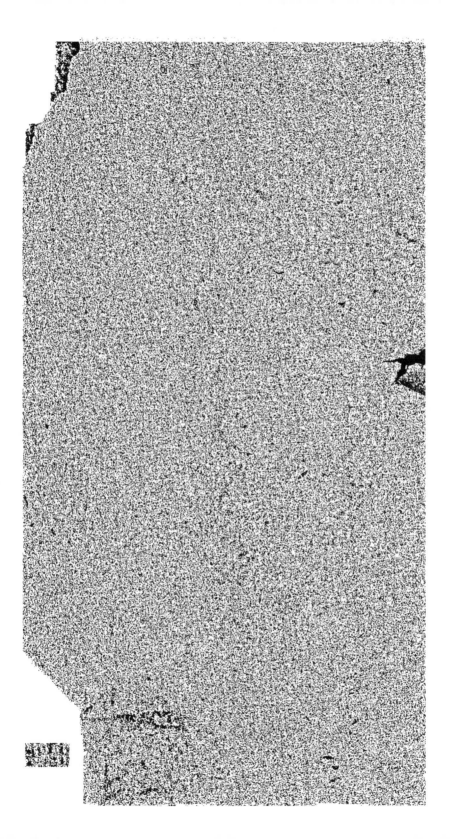

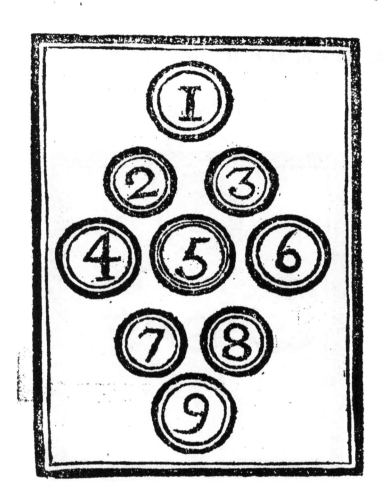

1. Boil'd Chickens.
2. Preferv'd Oranges or Apricocks.
3. Flummery.
4. Afparagus.
5. Lemon Poffet.
6. Roaft Lobfter.
7. Stew'd Apples.
8. Almond Cheefe-Cakes.
9. Lamb.

1. Cod's Head or Salmon.
2. Boil'd Chickens.
3. A fine Pudding or roaſt Lobſter.
4. Beans and Bacon.
5. Stew'd Breaſt of Veal.

1. Two young Turkeys or Ducklings.
2. Stew'd Apples.
3. Cuftards.
4. Jellies or Lemon Poffet.
5. Tarts.
6. Preferv'd Damfins.
7. Green Goofe or young Rabbits.

1. A Soop.
2. Scotch Collops.
3. Boil'd Chickens.
4. Stew'd Oyſters or roaſted Lobſter.
5. A Hunters Pudding.
6. Roaſted Tongue.
7. A Ham or roaſt Beef.
Remove. 1 Fiſh.

SECOND COURSE.

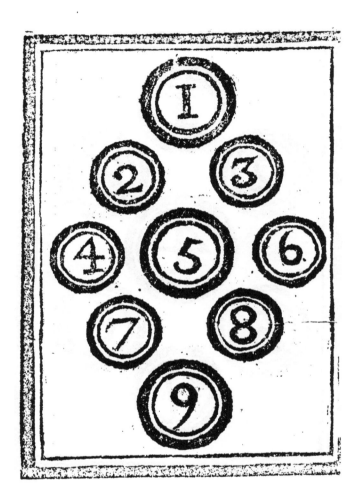

1. A Turkey.
2. Almond Cheese-Cakes.
3. Sturgeon.
4. Partridges.
5. Jellies.
6. A Hare or Woodcocks.
7. Collar'd Beef.
8. Cream Curds.
9. Ducks or Pig.

1. Gruel or Sack Poſſet.
2. Tarts.
3. Lobſter.
4. Jellies or Lemon Cream.
5. Solomon Gundie.
6. Cuſtards.
7. Boil'd Turkey with Oyſter Sauce.
Remove.   1. Wild Duck.

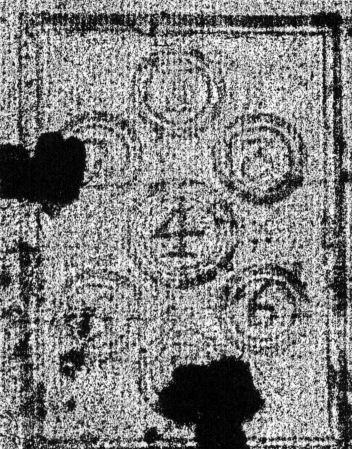

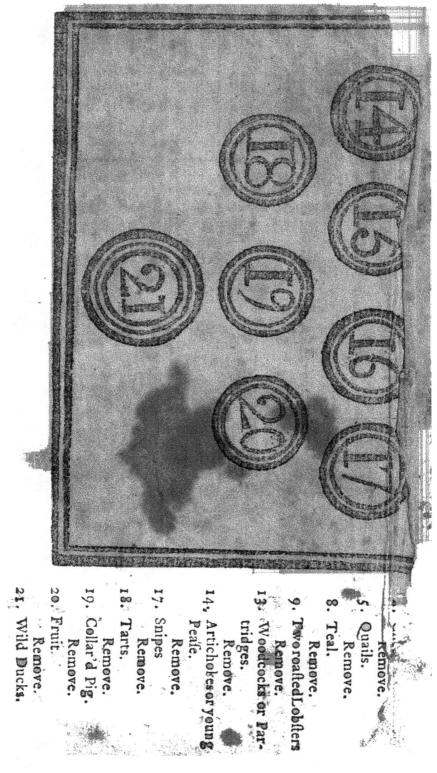

4. [illegible]
Remove.
5. Quails.
Remove.
8. Teal.
Remove.
9. Two roasted Lobsters
Remove.
13. Woodcocks or Partridges.
Remove.
14. Artichokes or young Pease.
Remove.
17. Snipes
Remove.
18. Tarts.
Remove.
19. Collar'd Pig.
Remove.
20. Fruit.
Remove.
21. Wild Ducks.

INDEX.

☞ Thofe mark'd [thus *] are in the Supplement.

M   Rich

I N D E X.

I N D E X.

INDEX.

I N D E X.

I N D E X.

I N D E X.

I N D E X.

Lightning Source UK Ltd.
Milton Keynes UK
UKHW012311171218
334172UK00017B/1734/P